Paradigms of the Church in Mission

Paradigms of the Church in Mission

A Historical Survey of the Church's Self-Understanding of Being the Church and of Mission

AUGUSTO RODRÍGUEZ

WIPF & STOCK · Eugene, Oregon

PARADIGMS OF THE CHURCH IN MISSION
A Historical Survey of the Church's Self-Understanding of Being the Church and of Mission

Copyright © 2012 Augusto Rodríguez. All rights reserved. Except for brief quotations in critical publications or reviews, no part of this book may be reproduced in any manner without prior written permission from the publisher. Write: Permissions, Wipf and Stock Publishers, 199 W. 8th Ave., Suite 3, Eugene, OR 97401.

Wipf & Stock
An Imprint of Wipf and Stock Publishers
199 W. 8th Ave., Suite 3
Eugene, OR 97401

www.wipfandstock.com

ISBN 13: 978-1-61097-469-1

Manufactured in the U.S.A.

To Anabella Rodríguez, my High School sweetheart and wife, for her support throughout the years of study and research; and to my children, David Andrés, Daniel Augusto, and Denisse Anabella, my three beautiful gifts from the Lord. To my parents, Porfirio and Lucy Rodríguez, who live in El Salvador, and to whom I owe so much for the values and morals they taught me. To Ministerios Nuevo Vivir, the congregation I pastor for their support and understanding. But most of all, to my Lord and Savior Jesus Christ for calling me into the ministry of the written word by sowing the seed for this book, and for providing everything according to his riches in glory.

Contents

List of Figures / viii
Acknowledgements / ix
Abbreviations / x
Introduction / xi

1. Paradigm Theory / 1
2. The Apostolic Paradigm / 18
3. The Christendom Paradigm / 31
4. The New Apostolic Paradigm / 45
5. A Transforming Revolution / 71
6. The Emergence of New Apostolic Churches / 105
7. Conclusions / 126

Bibliography / 141

Figures

Figure 1. Micro and Macro Paradigms / 6
Figure 2. Paradigm Changes and Paradigm Shift / 12
Figure 3. Augustine's Trifold Concept of the Church / 34
Figure 4. Centripetal and Centrifugal Mission of the Church / 43
Figure 5. The Ecology of the Church / 62
Figure 6. Charismatic Developments: A Timeline / 104

Acknowledgements

ALTHOUGH MANY PEOPLE HELPED in one way or another in shaping me through the process of my research and writing, I'm eternally grateful to my Lord and Savior Jesus Christ for his gift of salvation. I'm also thankful to many people who through their prayers and encouragement have also a part in this accomplishment; these are those faithful believers at Ministerios Nuevo Vivir.

I also want to extend my gratitude to Dr. Charles Van Engen for his inspiration and help through his teachings in theology of mission, and for his help in providing the initial steps to begin the writing process and his gracious recommendation to the publishers. To Wipf & Stock for believing in this project, to Christian Amondson because he was my first contact and in some way advocating for the vision of this book to become a reality.

Abbreviations

NIV	New International Version
NKJV	New King James Version
TEV	Today's English Version
Ign. Eph.	Ignatius, *To the Ephesians*.

Introduction

A SURFACE LEVEL READING of church history will let us see how the church has behaved throughout the centuries since its formation. However, just the reading will also bring questions about the different developments that took place within the church; such as, in the case of Acts 15, problems about evangelizing and reaching the gentiles.

We also see how believers in the early church took the Great Commission so seriously, as well as who were the first missionaries, the people of God. Later in history, we see a change in the role of the church and the empire. During this time there is also a change in the role of the clergy, the people of God, as well as a change in who were the missionaries.

Another important change we see in history is the Protestant Reformation of the sixteenth century. Once again, the role of the church changed as well as the role of the clergy and the role of the people of God. Of course changes took place, and in the last decade of the twentieth century another big change in the church occurred; a change that is still taking place that church leaders around the world are trying to understand.

As we read church history, we see different developments as a result of renewal movements in the church. These renewal periods which the church goes through, help clarify the vision and mission of the church, developing into revolutionary and cutting-edge congregations whose main purpose is to live out, as close as possible, the New Testament pattern of being the church.

In the early years of the twentieth century, the church experienced a transformation, a Holy Spirit experience similar to the one depicted by Acts 2:4. This gave rise to a Holy Spirit movement, and people related to it became known as "Pentecostals." During the 1960s, the church experienced a Second Wave of the Holy Spirit reaching mainline denominations, and later in the twentieth century, in the 1980s, a Third Wave of the Holy Spirit among historic denominational churches.[1]

The Second Wave or the Charismatic Movements, however, saw the birth of a number of churches and ministries that became independent of their denominations.[2] These churches have experienced a revolutionary transformation in their ecclesiastical structures, worship styles, mission and their understanding of being the church.[3] These churches are known as "Independent Charismatic,"[4] "New Paradigm Churches,"[5] or "New Apostolic Churches."[6]

The history of the church in mission has always been a struggle to carry out a two-sided commission, that of being a witness to the world, to convert and to save the world, and at the same time, to be different from the world.[7] Throughout the centuries the history of the church has been a history of changes. Different developments, changes in direction, power struggles, times of change and confusion, but with always one focus: mission.

I want to devote this study to those recent changes in the church. This study will help us to understand the different paradigm shifts that took place throughout history, and how they affected the church's self-understanding of being the church and of mission, the issue in focus is a historical survey of the paradigms of the church. Also in focus is the idea of mission, which has always been a challenge for the church.

THE RESEARCH PROCESS

I chose the process of historical research. In this process I used biblical studies, doing research and exegesis of passages from the book of Acts and other New Testament books dealing with ecclesiology, missiology, Christology, eschatology, pneumatology. This helped in developing, from a historical standpoint, an understanding of past important actions in

---

1. Burgess, et al., *Dictionary of Pentecostal and Charismatic Movements*, 2–3; Wagner, "The Third Wave," 844.
2. Pousson uses this term in *Spreading the Flame*, 17–18.
3. Wagner, *Churchquake*, 5.
4. Throughout his book Pousson uses this term to refer to this kind of churches.
5. Miller, *Reinventing American Protestantism*, 1, 13.
6. Wagner, "The New Apostolic Reformation," 18.
7. Mead, *The Once and Future Church*, 9.

mission in order to understand the present state of the church in mission and the emergence of its current expression, New Apostolic Churches.

Exegesis of some New Testament passages using primary and secondary sources has been essential. Sources like the Greek New Testament and other Bible translations (as needed), as well as all the necessary hermeneutical tools, with the purpose of understanding the theology of mission in first- and second-century apostolic church as well as the use of other early church writings.

The most adequate method for my research was historiography, the writing of history. This method helped me "think through issues of structure, pattern, and meaning"[8] as well as the proper use of resources and tools necessary to understand church history and historical missiology.

OVERVIEW

I have separated this study into different chapters dealing with the history of the church in mission. Chapter 1, entitled Paradigm Theory, provides a theoretical base for understanding paradigm theory, which helps us to understand the different paradigm shifts in the concept of being the church and of mission.

Chapter 2, The Apostolic Paradigm, provides a description of the newborn church's theology which would lead them into what they understood to be mission. Some theological perspectives that serve as basic assumptions and values forming the church's worldview are their understanding of Christ, of the Holy Spirit, their concept of the church, the role eschatology played in molding the church's mission, and of course, their concept of mission.

Chapter 3, The Christendom Paradigm, describes the changes in mission theology that took place after the conversion of Constantine and the end of official persecution. I examine the same theological perspectives in this paradigm to see how the concept of being the church also affected its concept of mission.

Chapter 4, The New Apostolic Paradigm, provides a description of the new and emerging paradigm. It explores the renewed theology of the NAP with respect to five major areas of theology: Christology, Pneumatology, Ecclesiology, Eschatology, and Missiology, as well as how this renewed theology is reflected in a renewed understanding of mission.

8. Shaw, "Introduction to Research Design."

Chapter 5, A Transforming Revolution, deals with recent secular and religious events of the late twentieth century that set the background for the emergence of the New Apostolic Churches.

Chapter 6, The Emergence of New Apostolic Churches, traces the events that mark the origin of this form of being the church as the current expression of the New Paradigm of the church in mission, and in chapter 7 I offer some concluding remarks.

This study will help in understanding the present state of the church as a result of a more recent paradigm shift, as well as tracing the emergence of the New Apostolic Churches, the current expression of the church in mission.

1

Paradigm Theory

LIVING IN A TECHNOLOGICAL age at the beginning of the twenty-first century, we cannot deny the fact that rapid changes are taking place around us. Neither can we deny the fact that those changes affect us in our way of living. Those changes have an impact on us as Christians and upon the church as well.

Due to the fact that rapid changes are happening all around people and all the time, they become resistant to changes in society. But the reality is that the world changes, people change, and culture changes around us. This raises a question: If the culture changes around us, does the church change? Of course this change does not mean a change in the church as the body of Christ in essence, but the question has to do with the changes in relationship to changes in culture.

Mike Regele reminds us that the invisible church, as such, lives outside and independent from culture. However, we cannot deny the fact that the church manifests itself in different eras and societies, as a social institution that reflects the norms of society and the beliefs of the culture where the congregation is ministering.[1]

It cannot be denied that the church is comprised of people who make up the culture, and as such, the church is affected by culture. Now, does this mean that the church as the body of Christ must adapt to the culture and live according to the culture? I believe so. Otherwise the church becomes irrelevant to the culture and the society it serves.

---

1. Regele, *Death of the Church*, 37.

In order to understand the historical developments of the church's self-understanding of church and mission, it is important to understand certain terminology that is widely used in today's world. I'm referring to the wide use of the term "paradigm."

When we apply paradigm theory to social science or missiology, we must try to understand why changes take place. From an anthropological point of view, we say that when people begin to question basic assumptions, changes begin to take place. That is when our worldview begins to change. Therefore, an understanding of worldview, its functions and how worldview is at the base of paradigm theory, is important.

UNDERSTANDING WORLDVIEW

The concept of paradigm gained recognition especially among the scientific community after the publication of Thomas S. Kuhn's *The Structure of Scientific Revolution* (1970). Kuhn, a physicist and scientific historian, limits his theory of paradigms to the natural sciences.[2] However, as Bosch says, Kuhn's theories are of great importance in today's changing world, changing "from one way of understanding reality to another."[3]

Worldview Defined

Worldview is at the core of culture. It is the nerve system of culture, out of which the conceptualizations of reality by the members of a given culture ascend. Charles H. Kraft defines worldview "as the culturally structured assumptions, values, and commitments/allegiances underlying a people's perception of reality and their response to those perceptions."[4] Kraft also says that worldview is inseparable from culture, but that "it is included in culture as the structuring of the deepest-level presuppositions on the basis of which people live their lives."[5]

Because worldview lies at the heart of culture, it touches every other aspect of culture.[6] This in turn will affect any conception, perception, or perspective of reality people have within a given culture. Worldview lies at the deepest-level of culture, conditioning the form the culture takes.

2. Bosch, *Transforming Mission*, 183–84.
3. Ibid., 185.
4. Kraft, *Anthropology for Christian Witness*, 52.
5. Ibid.
6. Kraft, *Christianity in Culture*, 83.

That is, people's behavior is shaped by their values, which stems out of their worldview.

Worldview is then a mental structure and a process. It is a structure because it shapes all different fields of knowledge; and a process because it integrates all various fields of knowledge, from theology to the culinary arts, "governing everyday behavior."[7] It is the basis of how people explain things happening in their life, how they ratify their beliefs and practices, as well as how they deal with problems that arise in an expected or unexpected way.[8]

Kraft's definition says that worldview includes assumptions. This must be understood as things that are not and were not written, but that they originated, presumably, by the members of the original group, who came into agreement at a given time. Later these assumptions were passed on to other generations, probably by different means, such as oral, written, or modeled to the young members of the people group.[9] A clear example of this is the case of the Hebrew people, who received the Law through Moses and were told to pass it on to other generations (Deut 6:5, 7).

Worldview Functions

Because worldview includes a set of assumptions and values, our commitments and allegiances will also be conditioned by our worldview. In other words, we will respond to any allegiance by making a commitment based on the worldview pattern we have learned in our culture. That is, we will evaluate, interpret and commit ourselves based on our perception of reality, which is not God's reality, which is complete, as opposed to ours, perceived according to our worldview.[10] It is ours, perceived according to our worldview.[11]

Worldview helps cultures to perceive reality, therefore worldview acts also as a lens through which cultures see and interpret reality. As in the case of a person wearing sunglasses, sometimes that person's view of

---

7. Hiebert, *Anthropological Reflections on Missiological Issues*, 11.
8. De Carvalho, "The Shaman and the Missionary," 5–6.
9. Kraft, *Christianity in Culture*, 53.
10. God's reality is complete, because He can see differently than what humans can. Paul says in 1 Corinthians 13:12 that at the present we see in part, and dimly, but God sees the totality. However, Paul adds, there will be a time when we all see as God sees and will know as God knows.
11. Kraft, *Anthropology for Christian Witness*, 52.

things may be impaired by the sunglasses, or the sunglasses may help that person to see better against the sun shining on his/her face. Worldview may condition the way we see things, because of the deep-level assumptions we have been taught, which will also become our guide in life.[12] In this way, worldview helps people to explain reality as they perceive it. That is, based on the assumptions we have at the deep-level we will explain what reality looks like.[13]

Worldview provides people with the basic assumptions and values to explain anything within their reality, such as philosophy, science, history, and matters of religion; theology, missiology, ecclesiology, and the like. Therefore, it does not matter if such explanations can be proven or not, because they are "assumed by people, they are part of their worldview."[14]

Worldview provides the means for interpreting, evaluating, and validating. The set of assumptions that lie at a deep-level of worldview will provide people with a way for interpreting things that are part of their reality. From the days of our childhood, we have been taught to interpret everything around us, from what is considered beautiful to what is considered as wrong, bad, or sinful. This does not only apply to the people of a given culture, but to families that make up the culture. Each family also has different worldviews from which they "educate"[15] their children.

For example, worldview helps people to interpret the meaning of words. Such is the case of foul words. One may ask, what are foul words? The answer will depend on people's worldview. Foul words in Costa Rica for example are not the same as those in El Salvador. Kraft says, "the assignment of meaning is a matter of personal interpretation based on social agreements concerning how to interpret cultural forms."[16]

Worldview influences the way people evaluate. That is, how people think reality ought to be. Worldview provides people with ways to judge things of their own reality. Evaluating goes hand in hand with interpreting and validating. Based on one's worldview, one assigns meaning

---

12. Ibid., 56.

13. Kraft, *Christianity with Power*, 184.

14. Ibid., 185.

15. Education in this context does not mean the type of education we are used to; that is, schooling. However, as Kraft says, education is the process of enculturalization, by which people learn how to behave and function as members of the society in which they are born (Kraft, *Anthropology for Christian Witness*, 274–75).

16. Kraft, *Anthropology for Christian Witness*, 60.

to things through the lens of worldview, which leads to how one values those things. This in turn will affect people's perception of ethics; good or bad, beautiful or ugly; religion, sinful or not, and many similar things.[17]

Because worldview helps to provide basis for evaluating, people's values will also be affected, and in turn, people's allegiances. According to people's worldview, people assign value to their commitments. Certain allegiances will have priority over others; therefore, people's commitments will also be affected.[18] The higher the value assigned on people's value scale, the stronger the allegiance, meaning a stronger commitment to that specific allegiance, making it more difficult for people to change.[19]

Worldview as Base for Paradigm Theory

Worldview provides a base for people to understand things: how they feel about things as well as how to valuate those things.[20] This will provide the people of a given culture with a way to function in their culture—knowing, feeling, and evaluating things from a given framework.[21] Paul G. Hiebert says that it helps the "reinforcement of systems."[22]

As I previously mentioned, worldview lies at the deep level of culture. The prior discussion on worldview and its functions is important because worldview provides the base for understanding and defining paradigm.

It is important to understand that worldview and paradigm are two different things, though related to each other. Paradigm emerges from worldview. However, worldview is made up of many paradigms, and many paradigms make up what is known as worldview.[23]

A different way for explaining this would be to consider micro- and macro-paradigms.[24] Micro-paradigms are the basic particles that make up worldview. As seen from our prior discussion of the definition

---

17. Kraft, *Christianity with Power*, 186.
18. Ibid., 189.
19. Kraft, *Anthropology for Christian Witness*, 61.
20. Hiebert, *Anthropological Reflections on Missiological Issues*, 36.
21. Kraft, *Anthropology for Christian Witness*, 58.
22. Hiebert, *Anthropological Reflections on Missiological Issues*, 36.
23. Kraft, *Christianity with Power*, 82.
24. Hans Küng uses the term macro-paradigm to refer to "major paradigms or fundamental models characteristic of whole epochs," and "micro-paradigms for many individual questions with which the various theologies have to deal" (see Küng, "What Does a Change of Paradigm Mean?," 214).

of worldview, worldview is made up of assumptions, values, commitments, and allegiances that condition how people behave. Each of these is in itself a paradigm. Kraft calls these "semi-independent 'picturings' or renderings of reality"[25]; the joining together of the micro-paradigms makes the worldview, and the whole makes a macro-paradigm.

Figure 1 shows how the joining together of different micro-paradigms form worldview. Just like bricks joining together make a wall, the joining together of micro-paradigms form worldview. The wall then becomes a macro-paradigm. Therefore, when one looks at culture, what one sees is the total sum of the many bricks together as the foundation of culture.

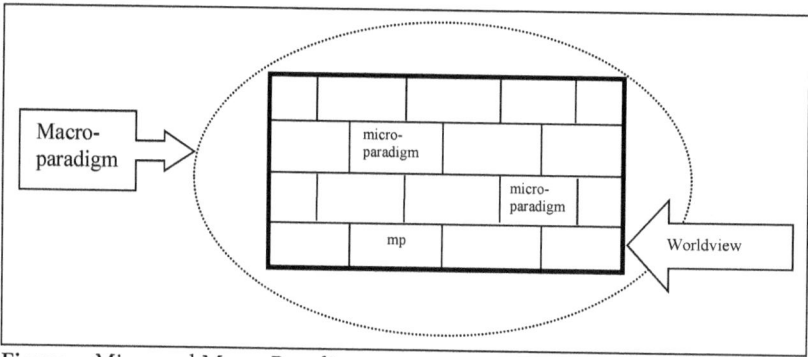

Figure 1. Micro and Macro Paradigms

In Figure 1, worldview is the finished wall, in which, once covered by plaster, one cannot see the bricks. This in turn is what makes a macro-paradigm. In Joel Arthur Baker's words this would be "forests of paradigms." In Baker's picture the forest seen from a distance looks like a big green blanket; but a closer look reveals the many trees that make the forest, which, in light of this study, represents a macro-paradigm. He considers that the interrelationship of all [micro]-paradigms is vital for the successful development in the long run of a culture.[26]

We can say, in a figurative way, that cultures are the ones that perceive reality in a given way, such that it differs from culture to culture, even though sometimes people of different cultures live in the same land, with only minor distance apart. I say that culture perceives reality, knowing that culture is made out of people. However, it is the people in a given

---

25. Kraft, *Christianity with Power*, 82.
26. Baker, *Future Edge*, 36–37.

culture who perceive reality according to their conceptualization (worldview) of what that reality should or should not be.[27]

DEFINING PARADIGM

The concepts of paradigm and paradigm shift are widely used in today's changing world of science, sociology, leadership, church studies, and missiology in general. However, if we don't have a clear understanding of what a paradigm is, we will not be able to understand paradigm shifts and how they affect cultures in their understanding of their present reality in order to act accordingly.

Etymology of the Word

A look at the dictionary will give us a common definition of paradigm. Paradigm comes from the Greek *paradeigma*, meaning pattern, model, or example, derived from the Latin *paradigma*, which in turns come from the Greek *paradiknynai*—to show side by side, compare (*para*—side by side, beside + *deiknynai*—to show, point out).[28] The idea of paradigm as "pattern" can be understood from the etymology of pattern, derived from old French *patron*—outline, model, plow; later meant model of behavior or appearance.[29]

Definition

Robert Paradowski, in an article for the *Survey of Social Science* (1994), a dictionary of sociology, says that "[a] paradigm refers either to an examplar or to a set of convictions shared by the members of a scientific community . . . also the constellation of beliefs, values, methods, theories, and laws shared by the members of a scientific community."[30]

When a given community holds a paradigm, people of that community are able to make sense of the phenomena they observe, also by helping the members of the community to solve puzzles that may come up. Nevertheless, it blinds people of that given community of other phenomena and puzzles that fall outside that given paradigm.[31]

---

27. Kraft, *Christianity in Culture*, 53.
28. Barnhart, "Paradigm," 754.
29. Ibid., 766
30. Paradowski, "Paradigm and Theories," 1328.
31. Ibid., 1329.

Key words in this definition are "set of convictions shared" as well as "the constellation of beliefs." Both these have to do with worldview shaping culture and in combination with micro-paradigms forming a paradigm of science; if we consider the fact that the members of a scientific community are actually a culture by definition, from an anthropological point of view.

Ed Oakley and Doug Krug in *Enlightened Leadership: Getting to the Heart of Change*, say, "contemporary behaviorists and sociologists use this word [paradigm] to describe any idea or set of ideas that provide the basis for a framework of beliefs and actions." In their own words, they consider that "a paradigm is a controlling perception—a mindset."[32]

Baker in *Future Edge: Discovering the New Paradigms of Success* defines paradigm as "a set of rules and regulations (written or unwritten) that does two things: (1) it establishes or defines boundaries; and (2) it tells you how to behave inside the boundaries in order to be successful."[33]

In this definition we also see how worldview plays an important role on paradigm theory giving shape to a paradigm. According to Baker, a paradigm shows people how to behave within a given paradigm by setting the rules of the "game." In fact, Baker considers that one's field of expertise is a paradigm, because people know how to behave within that field.

Baker uses the metaphor of games to illustrate paradigms, because all games have rules and regulations.[34] I think that what Baker refers to as paradigms (in the field of expertise or games) are in fact micro-paradigms, parts of the whole, because one's field of expertise or a game one plays are conditioned by the present worldview of the culture one is living in.

Nevertheless, I have to agree with Baker that paradigms do set the rules and regulations, because they are based on the present worldview. See Figure 1, where the frame of the macro-paradigm and micro-paradigms are representatives of the boundaries of how people behave according to how they perceive reality.

Hiebert in *Anthropological Reflections on Missiological Issues* refers to paradigms as "belief systems." Hiebert says that "belief systems select a domain of reality to examine, determine the critical question to be

---

32. Oakley and Krug, *Enlightened Leadership*, 97.
33. Baker, *Future Edge*, 32.
34. Ibid., 37.

investigated, provide methods of investigation, and integrate one or more theories into comprehensive system of beliefs."[35]

Baker says that paradigms set boundaries.[36] In similar way, Hiebert says that "beliefs systems set the boundaries for inquiry and determine the legitimacy of the problems examined.[37] Because worldview is conditioned by micro-paradigms, worldview helps people to solve any arising problem, "expected or unexpected."[38]

In this way, paradigms give an explicit meaning to worldview assumptions that lie beneath a culture. These assumptions are manifested or expressed in people's behavior: interpreting, based on feelings about the problem affecting people's lives, evaluating the facts, and taking action to solve the problem.[39]

Kraft simply defines paradigm as "a perspective on a sizable segment of reality."[40] The sizable segment of reality is the macro-paradigm, which is the result of the addition of micro-paradigms plus worldview (see Figure 1).

Considering the previous definitions of paradigm, I'd like to offer my own. Based on the understanding of micro-paradigms beneath worldview and together forming a macro-paradigm or what is commonly known as paradigm:

A paradigm is a cultural perspective of how people perceive and act according to reality, based on a framework of a given worldview, which in turns sets the boundaries for that given reality.

According to the previous study and my definition, a paradigm is not space. It is limited neither to geographical or physical boundaries, but to cultural ones. Therefore, I can say that paradigm is more related to time than to space. Cultures are not limited to space nor to geographical boundaries, however they are conditioned, and molded/changed with or by time.

This is in line with Charles E. Van Engen's definition that "[a] paradigm is a conceptual tool to perceive reality and order that perception

---

35. Hiebert, *Anthropological Reflections on Missiological Issues*, 37.
36. Baker, *Future Edge*, 32.
37. Hiebert, *Anthropological Reflections on Missiological Issues*, 37.
38. De Carvalho, "The Shaman and the Missionary," 6.
39. Hiebert, *Anthropological Reflections on Missiological Issues*, 37.
40. Kraft, *Christianity with Power*, 82.

in an understandable, explainable, and somewhat predictable pattern."[41] Furthermore, Van Engen considers that a paradigm is not a single concept, but a composite one. It is: "The composite set of values, world-view, priorities, relationships, spiritual insights, knowledge which makes a person, a group of persons, or a culture look at reality in a certain way. A paradigm is a tool of observation, understanding, and explanation, an epistemological foundation which takes into account the sum-total of definitions determining the way we perceive our reality."[42] Based on this, a macro-paradigm would be a specific period of time in history, where people of different cultures would behave and act according to how they perceive their present-time reality.[43]

DEFINING "PARADIGM SHIFT"

Bosch's analysis of Kuhn's theory "in a nutshell" is that knowledge grows by way of revolutions, when some individuals begin to perceive reality differently from their predecessors and contemporaries. When a person, or group of people, begins to question basic assumptions their worldview begins to change. At this time, people begin to look for "a new model or theoretical structure, or (Kuhn's favorite term) new 'paradigm'" that then begins to replace the old one.[44]

New paradigms are not the intentional result of a person or group of people. Nevertheless, they grow from "within the context of an extraordinary network of diverse social and scientific factors."[45] In the case of natural science, scientific factors play an important role in the changing of paradigms. Such is the case of new discoveries or proof of theories with the use of new technology.

Worldview Change and Paradigm Shift

Paradigm changes/shifts have their beginnings at worldview level. That is, paradigms begin to change when people's worldview begin to change.

---

41. Van Engen, "Theologizing in Mission," 55.

42. Ibid.

43. Hans Küng considers that a glance at historical theology will show the different paradigm changes there have been in the different periods of the history of theology and the church (Küng, "What Does a Change of Paradigm Mean?" 214–19).

44. Bosch, *Transforming Mission*, 184.

45. Ibid.

Paradigm Theory 11

Deep-level changes at this time have already begun to take place at the micro-paradigm level. People begin to revise the meaning of things according to their set of assumptions and values, and even though the end product of change will be a radical one, it is usually slow. However, the "transformational" process has already started.[46]

The term "paradigm shift" is widely used, however, I think there is a difference between paradigm change and paradigm shift. Considering the previous study of worldview as related to paradigm theory, paradigms are made of micro- and macro-paradigms, and before there is a paradigm shift, there must be a paradigm change.

A paradigm shift begins at the deep-level, affecting the roots of culture, the worldview level. This transformational process, as Kraft calls it, is a "matter of change in the central conceptualizations (worldview) of a culture."[47] These changes at worldview level begin a revolution of the culture, throwing everything out of balance in a culture.[48]

Worldview functions as a means to interpret, to evaluate and to act. Therefore, the transformational process will begin with a change of allegiance, a change in the way of evaluating things, and a revision of the behavior.[49] Beliefs and practices go together. Beliefs are part of the worldview, and any person would have to start by changing his/her beliefs before one can start changing his/her practices.[50]

In the gospel of Matthew chapters 5–7, we see Jesus introducing first century Jews to a paradigm shift. We read for example in Matthew 5:17 "do not think that I have come to do away with the Law of Moses and the teachings of the prophets. I have not come to do away with them, but to make their teachings come true" (Today's English Version). As we can see, this is a change in the practice of the Law of Moses; however, the change must start by changing their beliefs.

This was a radical change. A change of allegiance from that of the tradition of the elders to the new perspective Jesus brought. This was not an easy process, because they were used to practicing the Law in a given

---

46. Kraft, *Christianity in Culture*, 345.
47. Ibid., 347.
48. Kraft, *Anthropology for Christian Witness*, 65.
49. Kraft, *Christianity in Culture*, 349.
50. Kraft, *Christianity with Power*, 85.

way for long time and "[h]abits of long standing are not ordinarily replaced rapidly or without some trauma."[51]

The change in one's beliefs begins when one begins to question what is already assumed. Assumptions, by definition are things not questioned. They don't need to be questioned, they are assumed. However, there is a time when the "old rules" hardly apply to the present practice. Then is when the questioning begins.

In order to define paradigm shift, it is important to understand the basic meaning of some words. The word change by definition means, "to alter" or "cause to be different." Shift on the other hand, means "to move" or "transfer from one place or position to another, to change position, direction or place."[52] Therefore, according to our theory, a paradigm change would be an alteration of the micro-paradigm, and a shift would be a transfer or move of the macro-paradigm as a whole (see Figure 2).

Based on my definition of paradigm, a paradigm shift is:

A change of worldview from a cultural perspective of how people perceive and act according to reality, to a new definition of the boundaries set by the new worldview.

In a more simple way, a paradigm shift is the resetting of the boundaries by a new worldview.

A paradigm shift is similar to a revolution. There are new rules to apply, different ways of acting and practicing the way of living; and most of all, our basic beliefs also shift.[53] We don't believe differently, we just have a new way of living and of being.

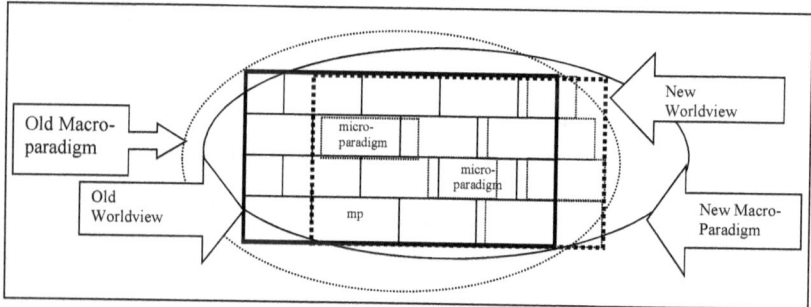

Figure 2. Paradigm Changes and Paradigm Shift

51. Kraft, *Christianity in Culture*, 346.
52. "Change," In *Encarta Encyclopedia on CD-ROM*, 1999.
53. Regele, *Death of the Church*, 185.

In Figure 2 we see that new micro-paradigms begin to push the old ones. This happens when basic assumptions at worldview level begin to be questioned by the people of the culture. Worldview begins to change because of pressure from the inside out, pressure that is usually associated with one's society. This pressure pushes people to develop new ways of understanding reality around them, and of course, changing the way they act.[54]

Figure 2 also shows the resetting of the boundaries. Because new mps begin to push old ones, a new boundary has to be set, which is a new worldview. This in turns pushes the old macro-paradigms (MP), ending in a totally new boundary. It is similar to movable partitions. They are movable walls that can be replaced by pushing them aside by new partitions. In Baker's portrait (see p. 6), it would be like a fire igniting the whole forest to give way to a newborn forest some time later. There will be other trees of the same kind, but they will be new ones making a new forest.

New paradigms begin to appear when the old ones are not able to solve present problems. That is, when the boundaries of the present paradigm are not big enough to help solve problems of the present state. Questions about the present state of things, such as technology or science and the rules and regulations by which people solve those problems do not allow for the right answer. It is the unsolved problems and the unanswered questions that work as trigger for a paradigm shift to take place.[55]

However, before a paradigm shifts there is a process. This process involves several stages: The first stage is that of denial. At this stage, people respond by denying what is challenged by the "existing paradigm." The next stage is that of an increase of evidence. As time goes by, people begin to see more evidence that something is not functioning well according to the present view of reality, and can no longer dismiss it. The forcing to fit into the new paradigm is the following stage. This is the stage when people of a given culture begin to bend the previous paradigm in order to fit into the new reality.

This is followed by a neglect to change. At this stage people have tried to bend the old paradigm, and because it does not work anymore they decide to shut themselves to a new possibility. This in turns leads to

---

54. Kraft, *Anthropology for Christian Witness*, 435.
55. Baker, *Future Edge*, 43–53.

a struggle to change, which is the next stage. Even seeing the problems arising and the difficulty of solving them under the old paradigm, people struggle with the new way of doing things; they have not accepted them yet. The last stage is acceptance, when enough evidence has accumulated to make it impossible to fit into the old paradigm any more. People change to a completely new way of seeing and understanding reality.[56]

Paradigm Changers

As I previously mentioned, changes begin from the inside of a culture, at the worldview level, because of pressure from within society.[57] Nevertheless, paradigms change and shift because there are certain people that help by advocating and implementing change. These are paradigm changers.

Baker considers four categories of paradigm shifters: new persons fresh out of training, the old ones shifting fields, the mavericks, and the tinkerers. The first two previously identified by Thomas Kuhn.[58] However, Baker says paradigm changers/shifters are usually outsiders.[59]

Paradigm changers can be classified within two major groups "advocates and implementors."[60] Advocates are those who bring change by convincing people of advantages of doing things in a new way. Implementors are the people who listen to the advocates and make the change.

Advocates of change may be outsiders who recommend change. They plant the seeds of change, help people by making them aware of the present situation and bring new ideas into a given culture.[61]

In Baker's categorizations,[62] the first category of advocates of change is persons fresh out of training. In a church situation, these can be recent seminary graduates with new and fresh ideas; they can be people who have recently experienced a renewal of their faith (which in reality is a stronger allegiance to Christ and his work; a worldview change leading to a paradigm shift).

---

56. How Paradigm Shift, www.tapestry.org/paradigmshift/html. Accessed February 9, 2001.
57. Kraft, *Anthropology for Christian Witness*, 435.
58. See Kuhn, *The Structure of Scientific Revolutions*.
59. Baker, *Future Edge*, 55–70.
60. Kraft, *Anthropology for Christian Witness*, 399.
61. Ibid., 399–400.
62. See Baker, *Future Edge*.

New persons coming out of training could also be those new in the life of the community. They could well be young men and women who are beginning to live life on their own. Regele considers that new generations are responsible for changes in society. In fact, Regele says there is a generational cycle responsible for changes in secular society as well as in the church. As example, Regele shows the different awakenings during the history of the church in North America. Apparently, "there is a regular and repeated cycle that is roughly eighty to ninety years in length."[63]

Older persons making a change of fields are also advocates of change.[64] They are new to a new field, and even though they are mature persons in life, they are inexperienced in the new field. Therefore "[t]hey don't realize they shouldn't challenge the present practices because they haven't learned those prohibitions yet."[65]

Implementors of change, on the other hand, are always insiders in a given culture. The process is of listening to the advocates, observing how things can be done differently, and then finally recommending the change.[66] Because they are insiders, they also become "role models" to others within the culture.

The other two categories proposed by Baker are the maverick and the tinkerers. These two fall within the implementors. Mavericks are those insiders who see problems within the present paradigm and know that by using the present paradigm they can't solve the problems. Therefore, mavericks raise questions about assumptions and values, and even though they operate and understand the present paradigm, they are not its captives.[67]

These people may be experienced pastors or missionaries who become frustrated with the present state of their work, operating under an old paradigm, and being ineffective, or not as effective as they would like to be, they seek new ways of doing their ministry. They're not afraid of trying new ways. They're not captives of the old paradigm.

The tinkerers, likewise the mavericks, see a problem and work under the old paradigm trying to solve it. Many times they can't. However, the

---

63. Regele, *Death of the Church*, 25–36.
64. Baker, *Future Edge*, 58.
65. Ibid., 59.
66. Kraft, *Anthropology for Christian Witness*, 400.
67. Baker, *Future Edge*, 64.

tinkerers are the ones who usually come up with new theories, or models of approaching a given problem.[68]

Effects of Paradigm Shifts

When a paradigm shifts, the boundaries are reset by the new worldview. However, there is time between paradigm shifts. During this time the waves of paradigms, the old and the new one, are felt. Both waves are rolling from different sources, but there is an inevitable time when both will crash with each other, and the crest will hit with a destructive power.[69] After an earthquake or a severe storm, everything is seen with different eyes.

A biblical example of a change of worldview and of paradigms is the case of Paul in his route to Damascus. He had a powerful encounter with the risen Christ and after Ananias prayed for him, Luke says in Acts, "something like fish scales fell from Saul's eyes, and he was able to see again" (Acts 9:18 TEV). Paul saw again, this time through a different worldview.

In a way, people in a new paradigm are forced "to look in a different direction."[70] However, people resist the change for fear of what the future may hold for them in the new paradigm, or fear of losing what has been already invented.

There are at least four effects of paradigm shifts, two positives and two negatives. Positive effects are: a) the ability to solve problems with a different perspective, and b) the feeling of being effective, as remuneration. On the negative side, a) one's status may change, providing the possibility of losing a social position, and b) one's title may disappear.[71]

In the following pages I will present a historical survey of the paradigm shifts that took place within the church's self-understanding of being the church and of mission. Having a better understanding of what a paradigm and a paradigm shift are, I will refer to the different epochs as "paradigms." David J. Bosch[72] uses the six epochs presented by Hans Küng; however, I will consider Loren B. Mead's divisions:[73] The Apostolic

---

68. Ibid., 65.
69. Regele, *Death of the Church*, 50.
70. Baker, *Future Edge*, 85.
71. Ibid., 69.
72. Bosch, *Transforming Mission*, 181–82.
73. Mead, *The Once and Future Church*.

Paradigm and the Christendom Paradigm, and I will use the name New Apostolic Paradigm for the last one.[74]

I will consider several aspects of the church's theological understanding in the different paradigms to compare and contrast how paradigms shifts in theology have also influenced the church's understanding herself and of mission.

---

74. Wagner, "Revival Power," 19, and Deiros, "Roots and Fruits of the Argentine Revival," 49, use this name to call the next stage in the church's life.

2

The Apostolic Paradigm

THE PREVIOUS STUDY OF worldview change and paradigm shifts is relevant to the following study of the church's self-understanding of being the church and mission. Considering the historical changes in theology, and, of course, the effects on the church and of her understanding of mission, the church is left with the option of learning from those changes.

The first paradigm is the Apostolic Paradigm, and it was forged during the first three centuries of Christianity, consisting of the first generation of disciples after Jesus' resurrection and up to the Edict of Milan in AD 313. It is apostolic not only because it covers the work of the church under the leadership of the original apostles,[1] but also because of the sending of the church; that is, the commission of the people of God (Matt 28:18–20).

Luke, the first church historian, tells us that Jesus took his disciples out of the city and blessed them as he ascended to heaven. In Luke's second volume, Acts of the Apostles, he tells us Jesus commissioned his disciples to be his witnesses in "Jerusalem, and in all Judea and Samaria, and to the end of the earth" (Acts 1:8 NKJV). In John 20:21 the commission is clearer; Jesus told his disciples "as the Father has sent Me, I also send you." This is known as the "apostolate of the church" or the "transferred apostolate."[2] Jesus transfers his commission to the next generation, his disciples, so they can continue the *Missio Dei*.

---

1. Petersen, *Church without Walls*, 67.
2. Van Engen, "Biblical Foundations of Mission," 122.

However, several perspectives of the newborn church's theology would lead them into what they understood to be mission, as well as how their understanding of mission was affected by their theology. Some theological perspectives that serve as basic assumptions and values, forming the church's worldview are their understanding of Christ, of the Holy Spirit, their concept of the church, the role eschatology played in molding the church's mission, and of course, their concept of mission.

CHRISTOLOGY IN THE APOSTOLIC PARADIGM

A way to study how the church understands Christ is by the different images the church uses to describe Jesus Christ. In the apostolic paradigm, a good place to start is in the gospels and how the gospel writers presented Jesus Christ to their readers.

Christology in the Gospels

Considering the different audiences to which the gospels were addressed, each gospel writer presented Christ in a different way. Matthew, having a Jewish audience in mind, presents Jesus as the "Messiah;" Mark, writing to a Roman audience, "people whose ideal was power and service," presents Jesus as the "Powerful Conqueror;" Luke, writing from a Greek paradigm, presents Jesus as the "Perfect Man," knowing that Greek philosophy was looking for the ideal man; finally, John, who has in mind the new heresies of his time, writes to Christians presenting Jesus as "God Incarnate."[3]

Matthew writes his gospel from a specific standpoint. Matthew cites the OT more than "several" times, in this way he shows how the life of Jesus of Nazareth fulfilled prophecy. The didactic elements of Matthew's gospel as lectionary and midrashic[4] show that his intentions were to teach his Jewish readers about Jesus the Messiah but also with the purpose that gentile believers could also profit from Jesus and his mission. This is seen in the final commission in 28:19: "make disciples of all nations."[5] Johannes Nissen[6] calls this "the Matthean Didactic Paradigm," where the missiological emphasis of disciple-making lies in a careful reading of the

---

3. Pearlman, *A Través de la Biblia*, 211.
4. Guthrie, *New Testament Introduction*, 32–38.
5. Tenney, *Nuestro Nuevo Testamento*, 190.
6. All references to Nissen are taken from an article published in Van Engen "Biblical Foundations of Mission," 399–403.

text in Matthew 28:19, where the main verb is "'to make disciples,' and going baptizing and teaching are subordinated to this discipling."[7] Hence, the goal of the mission here is to make disciples and "the [g]oing, baptizing and teaching" are as Wagner says "the helping verbs or the means toward the end of making disciples."[8]

The Gospel of Mark, the shortest of the gospels, directly presents the reader with the "gospel of Jesus Christ son of God." This, however, may mean the gospel Jesus preached or the gospel about Jesus Christ. Nevertheless, this would be a model for the church to continue the preaching (*kerygma*) "centered on the mission of the Son of God."[9]

One important characteristic of Mark's gospel is the fact that it is a historical narrative of the life of Jesus Christ. This in turns takes the reader to the "fast track" in the life and work of the Son of God, who is presented as the servant (Mark 10:45). The humanity of Jesus is one of the theological emphases in Mark, however showing the power that was with him in performing sings and wonders, which are also prominent in the gospel.[10]

Nissen considers "the Markan Paradigm" as the "Inclusive Kingdom and the Cross." The content of the gospel is "the coming kingdom of God." This is demonstrated by the different aspects of how the gospel should be preached, in teaching, performing healings, exorcisms, and calling and making disciples of all nations. The kingdom is present in the power and action to transform and confront.[11]

The journey motif is a special characteristic of this gospel (Mark 16:15). It is being on the way, as Nissen says. The two endings, considered by many NT scholars, have different missiological implications. The longer ending (16:9–20) implies a mission in action, that is, the continuance of Jesus' messianic mission (see Luke 4:18–19). Nissen calls this "triumphalistic in its character." The shorter ending, on the other hand, represents a theology of the cross and suffering. It has an abrupt ending

---

7. Nissen, "Paradigms of Mission in the Four Gospels," 395–403.
8. Wagner, *Strategies for Church Growth*, 50.
9. Harrison, *Introducción al Nuevo Testamento*, 179.
10. Martin, *The Four Gospels*, 220.
11. Nissen, "Paradigms of Mission in the Four Gospels."

because it is an invitation to the disciples of Jesus Christ to finish the "ongoing story of Christ's mission on earth—it is a mission on the way."[12]

Luke's Gospel is the proclamation of Jubilee.[13] The most important text in Luke is that of 4:16–30, as the proclamation of jubilee to the captives, the healing of the sick and of the brokenhearted. The social dimension of the gospel is of great importance, as it was in Jesus' ministry. Salvation is more than forgiveness of sin. It also includes a "total transformation of human life, healing from infirmities, and release from any kind of bondage."[14]

The social dimension of the gospel of Luke is also a way of saying that the mission is incarnational. This is also seen in the Gospel of John, which is presented from the beginning. Jesus, the divine *logos*, has become a human being who dwelt among the people (John 1:14). John's gospel is what Nissen calls "the Universality of Christ and the Incarnation."[15] At the end of the gospel we read of the transfer of the mission to the disciples (John 20:21), implying an incarnational mission of the disciples that is, an incarnational mission of the church.

Christology in the Pauline Corpus

In the Pauline corpus, Christology is seen in the many ways Paul refers to Jesus, as the "Christ, Lord, Son of God, Savior" and in his analogies to "Adam and wisdom."[16] Paul's understanding of Jesus as the Christ of God comes from his Judaic roots. In Jesus Christ, Paul had an understanding of his life and his world.

The Pauline corpus of letters serves as basis to understand not only Christology, but also many other theological perspectives of the early Christians. They saw Jesus Christ as the "apocalyptic Son of Man" who now had been "raised from the dead and who will soon return in glory to inaugurate the new age of God's kingdom."[17]

Paul explains Christology in a fourfold way, as with God before his birth, who lived on earth, ascended into heaven, and is waiting the time

12. Ibid.
13. Ibid.
14. Ibid.
15. Ibid.
16. Witherington III, "Christology," 100–15.
17. Placher, *A History of Christian Theology*, 39.

for his second coming.[18] This in turns dictates how the church in the apostolic paradigm understood themselves and their mission. The first two aspects show how the people of God would live on earth as the church of Jesus Christ, united with one another and to God through Christ; and the belief in the blessed hope of Christ's return to earth, meanwhile interceding for the saints.

The early Christians worshiped the one God, as did the Jews. However, the Lordship of Christ, as God revealed in the person of Jesus, helped them to develop the non-negotiable belief in the divinity of Jesus Christ Lord of all (Rom 9:5). Hence, Jesus is the Christ, but he is also the *Kyrios*, the Lord with supreme authority.[19]

Christology in the Apostolic Fathers

The term "apostolic fathers" usually refers to a group of Christian authors whose writings are from the end of the first and the beginning of the second century.[20] In 1672 the French scholar, Jean Cotelier, developed the term to refer to a group of writings that had both the simplicity and the same freshness of the apostolic writings of the NT canon.[21]

Christ is seen as God in the apostolic fathers, to the point that the historian Pliny the Younger says that Christians sing songs to "Christ as they sing to God." Christ is considered as preexistent and participant in creation. He is the Lord of heaven who will come back to judge the living as well as the dead. Christ is also present in the congregation of the church as they participate of communion.[22]

In the *Didache*, Jesus is presented as God and as mediator of God's glory and power. That is, the glory and power is given to God through Christ Jesus. However, Jesus is recognized as Lord, who has a day in which he is to be worshiped.[23] In *1 Clement*, Jesus is portrayed as the intercessor on behalf of believers. He is also seen as the "High Priest" whose name

---

18. Ibid.
19. Grenz, *Theology for the Community of God*, 71.
20. Hägglund, *History of Theology*, 15.
21. Sloyan, *The Jesus Tradition*, 13.
22. Hägglund, *History of Theology*, 20.
23. Sloyan, *The Jesus Tradition*, 14.

is to be invoked by believers. He is salvation for the lost and protector as well as helper for the weak.[24]

Ignatius of Antioch considers Christ as God incarnate in Jesus; that is, Christ in the flesh; and because of this, he is God and man. Ignatius does not try to explain the incarnation; however, he thinks that Christ, in taking the human form, remains one and the same.[25]

PNEUMATOLOGY IN THE APOSTOLIC PARADIGM

In the Apostolic Paradigm the Holy Spirit played a very important part in the overall mission of the church. Therefore, the importance of the Holy Spirit in the mission of the church lies in his role in the life of the believers. The Gospel of John presents a more defined treatment of the Holy Spirit. John sees the Holy Spirit as the divine *paraklete* (John 14:16–17). The Holy Spirit is another (*allos*) counselor. The idea of another counselor comes from the word *allos*, another of the same kind, of similar character. This means the Holy Spirit would be a counselor to the disciples as Jesus was.[26] Stanley Horton says that the word *parakletos* has the meaning of "a person called to help, counsel, or to advise someone," and even though one see the Holy Spirit as an advocate, we must also see the Holy Spirit as an intercessor.[27]

Luke, the first church historian, gives us some understanding of what early Christians thought of the Holy Spirit. In Acts 1:8 we read that the Holy Spirit is the one who would give Christians a dynamic power to be witnesses of Jesus Christ.[28] The Holy Spirit is also the one who fills the believer (Acts 4:5, 8). Early believers considered the Holy Spirit as

24. Ibid.
25. Bromiley, *Historical Theology*, 4; see also Ign. *Eph.*. 7:2, 29.
26. Vine, "Allos," 106–7.
27. Horton, *El Espíritu Santo Revelado en la Biblia*, 91–92.
28. In the Greek, the word used δυναμις (dunamis), has the meaning of ability, possibility and power, physical, intellectual, and spiritual. The *dunamis* of God on the disciples is for them to continue the work of Christ. In Pentecost, a special endowment of the Holy Spirit comes upon the believers, enabling them to boldly testify of the resurrection of Jesus Christ, and confirming this with signs and wonders, manifested in the form of healings, exorcisms and the preaching with power. The *dunamis* of God in the believers is both a manifestation of God's presence and the believers's existence. The preaching with the *dunamis* of God, accompanied by signs and wonders, is so unbelievers put their faith in the power of God and not in human wisdom. (1 Cor 2:1–5; Kittel and Friedrich, eds. "δυναμι, δυναμις," 187, 190–91).

empowering to testify, to perform works of faith in the form of healings, and encouraging believers to take the gospel to everyone (Acts 4:29–31).

The Holy Spirit also calls and sends people into ministry (Acts 13:1–3), as well as gives wisdom to church leaders to deal with difficulties arising with the inclusion of the Gentiles into the church (Acts 15:28). In fact, Paul, in 1 Corinthians 2:10–16, asserts that the only means God uses to communicate his wisdom to humans is through the Holy Spirit.[29]

As the source of dynamic power, Paul attributes his success in the mission to the power of the Holy Spirit in the working of signs and wonders that accompanied his preaching.[30] Paul also considers the Holy Spirit as the one who endows believers with spiritual gifts to accomplish their ministry, and that the role of the government gifts of Ephesians 4:11 is to help the people of God find their place in the Body of Christ, so they can do the work of the ministry (1 Cor 12:4–11).

The first generation of Christians considered that leadership should be charismatic. Charismatic in the sense that the Holy Spirit endows believers with gifts to do the work of the ministry. Therefore, the Holy Spirit could speak through anyone. As 1 Corinthians 14 shows, Paul is laying the foundations of how early Christians were to conduct the worship service.

Early believers not only asserted their belief in one God, the Father and in the Lord Jesus Christ, but they also believed God was present and among them in the person of the Holy Spirit. This was the result of a continuous personal experience with the divine Spirit, who was neither the Father nor the Son. In fact, the NT shows how the writers thought of the Holy Spirit in personal terms, by using masculine pronouns when addressing the Spirit.[31] They also attributed aspects of personality such as will, emotion and intellect. However, early believers never thought of the Holy Spirit as subordinate to the Father or the Son, but on the same level of divinity, which is seen in cases such as the Great Commission in Mt. 28:19 or the apostolic blessing of 2 Corinthians 13:14.[32]

---

29. Paige, "Holy Spirit," 406.

30. Ibid.

31. See for example John 16:8, 13–15 in which case the pronoun should be neuter since *pneuma* is neuter, John however used a masculine pronoun. 1 John 2:6; 3:3, 5–7 where the same pronoun is used to refer to God the Father.

32. Grenz, *Theology for the Community of God*, 72.

CONCEPT OF THE CHURCH IN THE APOSTOLIC PARADIGM

In the early beginnings, the church was a minority faith and considered only as a sect within Judaism, just like the Pharisees were (cf. Acts 26:5; 28:22). However, it was considered as *religio licita*[33] within the Roman Empire.[34] Early Christians understood themselves to be the *ekklesia*, the called-out of the world, living by the power of Christ through the Holy Spirit, according to Jesus' principles and values. They were conscious of who they were and of their commissioning to heal the sick, to serve, and to convert the world.

However, there were some questions about who they were in relationship to those around, if they were to be in the world, but not of the world (John 17:5). To whom were they sent? Who were the sick, the brokenhearted and the prisoners who needed deliverance? (Luke 4:16–18). The church as an institution had its boundaries clearly defined, because it was in the middle of everyday life that they answered these many questions. The church was living in a hostile world, and the militant church had its orders: to engage those in the world, and not to withdraw from them.[35]

In the Apostolic Paradigm, the church was made of a series of local congregations in a given city or region.[36] An example is the church at Corinth, many congregations in one city or the Galatian churches, many congregations spread out through the region of Galatia. Local congregations supported each other by different means, such as encouraging each other (Heb 10:23–25), providing financial support (Rom 15:25–26; 1 Cor 16:1–2) as well as engaging in mission together (Phil 2:24–25).[37]

---

33. Under Roman law certain religions were permitted to exist in the pluralistic society. Religions falling under this category were protected and accepted in the Empire, as long as they did not pose any threat to the welfare of the Empire. The Jewish religion, although unpopular, enjoyed this status, and as long as the Empire did not distinguish between Jews and Christians, Christianity was also tolerated (Martin, *The Four Gospels*, 27, 94).

34. Dunn, "Models of Christian Community," 1–18; Bosch, *Transforming Mission*, 191.

35. Mead, *The Once and Future Church*, 10–12.

36. By local congregations I mean congregations in a given place, either at Corinth as house churches forming the church in the city, or a series of house churches in a region, the Galatian churches.

37. Regele, *Death of the Church*, 187.

The Church as Community

James D.G. Dunn considers several models of the church as community in the NT. The first community to which Dunn refers is that of the first people Jesus called to follow him. Four characteristics identify this community: eschatological, because of the coming kingdom; discipleship, because of the people who followed Jesus, some literally, others in beliefs, remaining in their places. A third characteristic of this community is that it was open, meaning that it did not require any form of ritual of initiation for the followers. However, the most important characteristic of all is that it was centered in Jesus, depending totally on him.[38]

The church as seen in Acts did not confine the Spirit to a few, but all shared the same experience. As a matter of fact, those who did not have a personal experience with the Holy Spirit were encouraged to have it (Acts 8:15–17; 10:44–47; 19:6).[39]

Pauline Concept of the Church

There is yet another NT concept of the church, the Pauline concept of the church. Since Paul is responsible for most of the doctrine taught in the NT, his concept of church is important as well, especially when we consider the fact that his writings were first in circulating, even before the Gospels.[40]

Paul understood *ekklesia* as the assembly of the people of God, the assembly of the "full citizens" of the kingdom (Phil 3:20; Eph 2:19). Nevertheless, the people of God did not become *ekklesia* until they were assembled together. *Ekklesia* does not have to do with a particular place, but it surely is an indicative description of an identifiable object, the gathering of the people of God.[41]

The term *ekklesia* is used in the Septuagint, is later used by the first Hellenistic-Christians to refer to them. However, *ekklesia* denotes the whole people of God. But in Paul's case, he first used it to refer to local congregations, made of Christians gathering in one place, especially with reference to house churches, such as the case of Acts 16:15, 40, Romans

---

38. Dunn, "Models of Christian Community in the New Testament," 1–3.
39. Ibid.
40. O'Brien, "Church," 123–31.
41. Ibid., 123–25.

16:5, Colossians 4:15 and Philemon 2.[42] An important fact in this respect is that the Early Church did not own a place specifically for worship until the middle of the third century.[43]

The Church as a Charismatic Community

The concept of the church as a charismatic community has to do with Paul's view of the church as the Body of Christ (Rom 12; 1 Cor 12 and Eph 4). The church as a charismatic community is seen as a body, where everyone has an experience with the Holy Spirit and is endowed by the Holy Spirit with gifts to accomplish the mission. In this church there is no room for a one-person ministry, or a ministry confined to only one person doing all the work, or confined to a special group of people within the Body. This kind of church is characterized by unity among diversity. This is a church where every member functions in different ministries. It is only in this way that the charismatic community can be the Body of Christ.[44]

Paul, in using the image of the Body of Christ, shows the church as composed of many members who have a responsibility for the well being and the functioning of the Body (Rom 12:4–8; 1 Cor 12:12–31). Also important is the fact that the Head of the Body is Christ himself, the one who leads the church (Eph 1:20–23), not anyone in the government of the church, such as apostles, prophets, evangelists, or pastors-teachers (Eph 4:11).

The Pauline idea of the household of God considers every member of the family with a function. God is the Father and the *adelphoi* (brothers and sisters) are the children of the house. However, the household image goes beyond the people, because there are certain utensils used for different purposes in the house. Paul says there are dishes and bowls, some made of gold, some made of silver, and some made of wood. Each one is used for different tasks; nevertheless, gold utensils are used for special occasions, others for ordinary use (2 Tim 2:20 TEV). The idea here, as well as with the Body, is that each member of the household is of use, and

---

42. Bosch, *Transforming Mission*, 165; Dunn, "Models of Christian Community in the New Testament," 6; O'Brien, "Church," 125.

43. O'Brien, 125.

44. Dunn, "Models of Christian Community in the New Testament," 6–8.

must be clean and pure in order to be used by the Head of the household for every good work (2 Tim 2:21).

ESCHATOLOGY IN THE APOSTOLIC PARADIGM

Eschatology played an important role in the early developments of the church in mission. Three basic reasons: eschatology calls to sanctification, gives a sense of victory and produces a sense of urgency.

Eschatology Calls to Sanctification

The sense of the imminent coming of the Lord moved believers to sanctify themselves, to be holy by surrendering to God "your whole being to him to be used for righteous purposes" (Rom 6:13, 19, 22 TEV). Sanctification is then a consecration to God, and to truly represent God among all people's, therefore calling all believers to be holy as God is also holy (1 Pet 1:16; 4:17). In Romans 13:11–14, Paul calls believers to "awake out of sleep" (NKJV) and to walk properly, especially because the coming of the Lord is near. To the Thessalonian believers Paul tells them that sanctification is the will of God (1 Thess 4:3).

Eschatology Produces a Sense of Victory

A clear expression of the sense of victory in the Early Church is worship. They worshipped on Sunday because it was the day the Lord was raised from the dead. This is important, because of the eschatological element. The Early Church celebrated the resurrection, not the death and crucifixion, of Jesus Christ.[45] The sense of victory came from the understanding that the battle was already won by Jesus Christ at Calvary, although the ratification of victory will not come until the consummation of the kingdom.[46] However, in light of the present time sufferings Paul says, "we are more than conquerors through Him who loved us" (Rom 8:37 NKJV).

It is the resurrection of Jesus, which gives the sense of victory, knowing that, as Jesus was raised from the dead, all who believe in Him will also rise. Therefore, the proclamation is now that Jesus was raised from the dead and He is the first-fruits. All believers will follow. This gives hope, hope that is not seen, but hope that final victory is at hand (2 Cor 4:16–18; cf. 1 Cor

---

45. González, *Historia del Cristianismo*, Vol. 1, 37.
46. Bosch, *Transforming Mission*, 142.

15:55–57). This is the reason why all believers should work for the Lord always, knowing that "your labor is not vain" (1 Cor 15:58).

Eschatology Produces a Sense of Urgency

Jesus has not only died, but He has been resurrected and soon will return to consummate the kingdom. In the meantime, it is the church's responsibility as the Body of Christ on earth to be Jesus' hands to touch the needy; his feet to go where the need is; his eyes to see how he sees, with no partiality; and most of all, to be his heart, to love as he loves.

The imminent return of Christ in power and glory is the reason why the church in worship exclaims, "come Lord Jesus" *Maranatha* (1 Cor 16:22; Rev 22:17). This imminent return is intensified in this paradigm as oppose to Jewish apocalyptic thinking of the OT.[47] This also makes Paul compel every person to accept God's grace, because it is "now the accepted time, now is the day of salvation" (2 Cor 6:2 NKJV). Paul himself feels this urgency to fulfill the mission to the point of saying "how terrible it would be for me if I did not preach the gospel!" (1 Cor 16:9 TEV). This should not be understood as a heavy burden for Paul, but coming out of that sense of the immediate return of Christ.[48]

MISSIOLOGY IN THE APOSTOLIC PARADIGM

The Apostolic Paradigm considers the church's mission as its base. Therefore, the primary focus of the church in mission is the proclamation of the Gospel—it is to give testimony of the risen Christ. That was their understanding of the Great Commission—to communicate to the world the resurrection of Christ and the resurrection power.[49]

The church's understanding of mission was the same as the one Jesus gave to his disciples: proclaim that the kingdom of God is near, "heal the sick, raise the dead, cleanse those who have leprosy, drive out demons" (Matt 10:7–8 NIV). In this paradigm the church considered their mission field as the world, and that all believers were participants in the mission. As a matter of fact, they considered their mission frontier being the neighborhood (Acts 1:8; 2:46–47).[50]

---

47. Ibid., 143.
48. Ibid., 133–39.
49. Van Engen, "Biblical Foundations of Mission," 117.
50. Mead, *The Once and Future Church*, 12.

All believers were endowed with spiritual gifts and empowered by the Holy Spirit to carry out the specific task of the church (1 Cor 12:7–11). All of them understood they had authority in the name of the Lord to do the work of ministry (John 20:23; Acts 3:16) by proclaiming and demonstrating the power of the kingdom of God in healing the sick, raising the dead, and casting out demons.[51]

The training of the people of God for mission was not conducted in special schools, but at the local congregation and by church government level ministers ministers (Eph 4:11–12). There were no special schools of training for church leaders, pastors, or missionaries as in the modern sense of seminaries. However, they had schools of leaders (Acts 19). We read in the NT that Jesus told his contemporaries what his mission was, and then he sent them to do as they had seen him do (Luke 4:18–19; Mt. 10:8).

The way training was conducted was by apprenticeship, where the disciple learns by seeing what the teacher does, and then he/she does it. We can see this in Paul's ministry, for example, when he tells the Corinthians to imitate him (1 Cor 4:16; 11:1). In 2 Timothy 2:2 his counsel is to "take the teachings that you heard me proclaim in the presence of many witnesses, and entrust them to reliable people, who will be able to teach others also" (TEV).

The church's life and their reason for being were defined by their everyday life in the mission frontier. Their task was to involve each member by teaching them how to do ministry, encouraging them, and giving them skills to effectively communicate the Gospel in order to multiply themselves into several missionaries.[52]

Every member understood that everyone was to be involved in mission, and the power to take the mission—crossing boundaries—came not from themselves but from the Holy Spirit. This is the reason why the church of the Apostolic Paradigm also had the structures and the roles of each member of the Body in place, so they could do that kind of mission.[53]

---

51. Deiros, "The Roots and Fruits of the Argentine Revival," 46–47.
52. Mead, *The Once and Future Church*, 12.
53. Ibid., 13.

3

The Christendom Paradigm

A TYPICAL MISUNDERSTANDING OF the use of the terms Christianity and Christendom raises the need to clarify these concepts, especially in the way I use the concept of Christendom. It is very common for the untrained to use both terms interchangeably to refer to the same thing. For example, the dictionary in Encarta Encyclopedia 1999 on CD ROM, defines Christianity as "the Christian religion founded on the life and teachings of Jesus." Christendom is used to refer to all Christians collectively or the Christian world.

Nevertheless, Christianity and Christendom are two different concepts. Christianity, as previously mentioned, is the Christian religion. Christendom, on the other hand is a "cultural reality" derived from Christianity.[1] Enrique Dussel defines Christendom as a political, economical, and ideological reality that has its base in the church as means to justify the system; and where the church uses the state as means to fulfill its mission, as well as establishing an allegiance with the socio-political dominant classes.[2] As a cultural reality, Christendom teaches people how to behave, what to say, and how to say it. It has its own system of values and assumptions, as well as allegiances and commitments.

At first, Christendom established a fixed liturgy; there was no room for diversity in the "new empire." People filled the basilicas. They were baptized, and without any instruction, were entrusted with "serious responsibilities toward history." Many were baptized as children and

---

1. Dussel, *History and the Theology of Liberation*, 70.
2. Dussel, *Historia General de la Iglesia en América Latina, Tomo 1*, 174–75.

automatically became part of the church without a personal conviction of repentance from sin, contradicting in this way the gospel message (John 3:5, 2 Cor 5:17), and of course the mission of the church as well. Christendom also used the state as means to fulfill the mission. Bishops who were under persecution before became important authorities in the new empire.[3]

It is in this fashion that I will use Christendom to understand the next paradigm in the history of the church in mission. As seen from this brief definition of Christendom, the church's self-understanding of being the church and of mission will drastically change in comparison with the Apostolic Paradigm.

THE BEGINNINGS OF CHRISTENDOM

By the end of the second century and the beginnings of the third persecution of Christians has diminished. In AD 303, Diocletian proclaimed an edict ordering the destruction of Christian places of worship and the burning of sacred books; highly ranked Christian officials were demoted and those who did not recant their faith were taken as slaves. Finally, on April 30, 311 AD, Galerious on his death-bed proclaimed the Edict of Toleration which, among other things, mentioned the publication of the prior edict to persecute those who did not conform to the "Ancient institutions, many of those were brought to order through fear, while many were exposed to danger . . . with our wonted clemency in extending pardon to all, are pleased to grant indulgence to these men, allowing Christians the right to exist again and to set up their places of worship."[4]

In AD 312, Constantine began his march to Rome against Maxentius Caesar. The pagan Maxencius needed all the power he could get from pagan magic. However, he felt a stronger power against him. Constantine, before confronting Maxentius at the famous battle over the Milvian Bridge, had a vision where he was ordered to put a Christian symbol as emblem for the battle. In his vision, Constantine saw a cross in the sky with the inscription "By this you shall conquer." Constantine then

---

3. Dussel, *History and the Theology of Liberation*, 70–71.

4. Lactantius, *De mort. pers.* XXXIV: 3–4, *Edict of Toleration*, 311; see also González, *Historia del Cristianismo*, Vol. 1, 119–23 and Latourette, *Historia del Cristianismo*, Vol. 1, 129–30.

changed the Roman emblem to that of the Greek letters Chi and Rho, the first two letters in the name *christos* in Greek.[5]

In AD 313, Constantine and Licinius, who at the time were both emperors, met at Milan and proclaimed the Edict of Milan that ended all persecution of Christians. The Edict of Milan marks the beginning of Christendom. However, Constantine's sons, who succeeded him in the Empire, supported the Christian faith in a stronger way than their father. Christian communities grew faster. People wanted to become Christians not because of personal convictions, but for other reasons, such as official favor, riches, and peace, instead of persecution.[6] Christendom had officially begun.

CHRISTOLOGY IN THE CHRISTENDOM PARADIGM

In Christendom, the way of viewing Jesus has changed. No longer seen as the victorious Christ of the resurrection, but as the suffering Christ of the crucifixion. In the Apostolic Paradigm, the church met to celebrate Jesus' resurrection; in Christendom it is to remember his crucifixion, that is, his death.

In the Apostolic Paradigm, Jesus' miracles were to be performed by his followers. In Christendom, they are considered as fulfilling a purpose during a specific period of time, the apostolic period, if not doubted completely, because the focus is to study Jesus' work, and not to continue his mission. Jesus' mission is to be studied for the sake of understanding it, and not for the purposes of continuing it.

This is clearly seen by the different views of Christ. Gnosticism, for example considered that Christ brought salvation knowledge. However, he was a spiritual Christ and only appeared to have a physical form.[7]

In the Christendom Paradigm, Christology becomes an aspect of salvation. Christ is salvation, but the emphasis is on understanding salvation and the atonement; it is to study and develop a sound doctrine of the atonement. Examples of this are Anselm of Canterbury and Peter Abelard.[8]

---

5. González, *Historia del Cristianismo*, Vol. 1, 123; Latourette, *Historia del Cristianismo*, Vol. 1, 131.

6. Latourette, *Historia del Cristianismo*, Vol. 1, 133.

7. Hägglund, *History of Theology*, 37–38; Placher, *A History of Christian Theology*, 47.

8. Placher, *A History of Christian Theology*, 142–48; Bromiley, *Historical Theology*,

Through the Reformation, theologians continued studying Christology, each giving their own understanding, however, never contradicting Scriptures. Christology was absorbed by soteriology. Emphasis was on Christ's work on behalf of humanity. Therefore reflection should be on Christ's work on Calvary.[9]

THE CHURCH IN CHRISTENDOM THEOLOGY

During the time of the persecution under Galerious, many Christians were forced to recant their faith and turn in sacred Scriptures. Those who recanted and turned in Scriptures were considered as traitors. This unleashed the Donatist controversy, a schism named after the bishop of Carthage, Donatus the Great.[10]

Augustine of Hippo, in opposing the Donatists, developed his concept of the church, which helped to understand the church during Christendom. Augustine thought of the church in three aspects: the external organization (the institution)—Christendom; the communion of the saints—those who have received salvation through Christ, including the ungodly and the hypocrites, even if they have the spirit of love; and the elect—those who share the grace and will be faithful until the end (Figure 3).

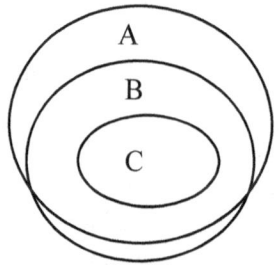

A. The External Organization, Christendom
B. The Communion of the Saints
C. The Elect

Figure 3. Augustine's Trifold Concept of the Church

Figure 3 above explains Augustine's idea of the church. Christendom (A), involves the communion of the saints (B) plus the elect (C), those in the middle. However, the total sum is what in Augustine's idea Christendom is. In the Christendom Paradigm, the problem is with

---

111–12; 178–79.

9. Sloyan, *The Jesus Tradition*, 73–76.
10. Hägglund, *History of Theology*, 124.

respect to Augustine's idea of the church as the "City of God," presented in of one of his books. Here he identifies the church—the communion of the saints ("B" in Figure 3) with the kingdom of God.[11] Augustine also thought that the final outcome should be that of the "City of the World" becoming part of the kingdom, the kingdom being the final objective and the earthly state should fulfill its purposes as a truly Christian state.

It is this line of thought in the Middle Ages that leads people to believe that the State should be subject to the church. During this time all people within the limits of the empire were free to practice their religion, and the Edict of 324, where by an imperial order all soldiers should worship the Supreme God on the day of the Sun, gave the impression that church and state were the same. Therefore, emperors and kings received their power from the pope.[12]

Following this same line of thought, everybody who belonged to the church was also in the kingdom of God. The church was the clergy and the hierarchical organization was the manifestation of the fellowship of all believers.[13] If anyone dared to leave the church, that person would also leave the kingdom. Belonging to the church was the order of the day. Authority and holiness were attributed to those adhering to the institutional church, even if they did not give any evidence of such virtues.[14]

The institutionalization of salvation was evident by this time. Being part of the institutional church was equal to being saved. Therefore, the church was the means for salvation and not Jesus' death and resurrection. It was inhuman to be outside the church and the Empire, and someone outside the church was also an outlaw. Treason and heresy were similar things.[15]

Martin Luther had a similar view of the church as that of Augustine. Although Luther did not mention three aspects of the church, two were clearly defined: An "inner fellowship" of those on earth, and the external fellowship, those assembled in a given place, belonging to a parish or diocese. This is the external Christendom, made out of those who have received the Word and confess their faith, however without a clear

---

11. Ibid., 131.

12. González, *Historia del Cristianismo, Vol. 1*, 140–41; Hägglund, *History of Theology*, 131–32.

13. Hägglund, *History of Theology*, 132.

14. Bosch, *Transforming Mission*, 218.

15. Mead, *The Once and Future Church*, 16.

demarcation of believers and hypocrites.[16] Luther's view provides for considering anybody belonging to a parish or diocese as members of the church, either by the "minister of the Word" or by themselves. Anyone living around the geographical reach of the local congregation belonged to that congregation, and to the church.

However, a strong point in Luther's view of the church is the priesthood of all believers. He thought that all believers were competent in any matter regarding the faith, as well as having the right to have and the duty to interpret the Scriptures by themselves. Nevertheless, in Luther's view not all believers had the ability to perform the work of the ministry (Eph 4:12) but only those of the second order, the Office State; those of the Christian State were not able to administer the Word and the Sacraments.[17]

Sometime later, John Calvin would have a similar view. Inspired by Augustine's view of the church, Calvin thought that church and state should function together, to the point of attempting "to make the city of Geneva a model of this cooperation."[18]

In Christendom, being a Christian was a matter of tradition. It was something obvious, handed down from generation to generation. Conversion did not have anything to do with being a Christian, because one was born into Christianity. People became members of the church by infant baptism, and everybody would have their children baptized.[19]

However, the same applies to many people in today's Christian world. Some are raised Roman Catholics, others, Protestants, but many don't have a conversion experience. They were and are born into Christendom. What is important to point out is the fact that the Christendom Paradigm is still in practice, even though overlapping the new and emerging paradigm.

PNEUMATOLOGY IN THE CHRISTENDOM PARADIGM

During the Christendom Paradigm, the emphasis was on the church as an institution. The Holy Spirit was the one who illuminated and purified the believer, but everything was centered on the church. The Holy Spirit

---

16. Hägglund, *History of Theology*, 244–45.
17. Petersen, *Church without Walls*, 101; Hägglund, *History of Theology*, 246.
18. Hägglund, *History of Theology*, 264; see also Petersen, *Church without Walls*, 102.
19. Dussel, *History and the Theology of Liberation*, 71; Petersen, *Church without Walls*, 106; Mead, *The Once and Future Church*, 16.

did not play any role in the outward mission; the church had entered the inward-looking state.[20]

In the Apostolic Paradigm the Holy Spirit endows believers with the *dunamis* of God for effective witness; whereas, in the Christendom Paradigm, because persecutions had ended, there was no need of a "supernatural power" to engage in mission. Mission was to be conducted by the empire through the soldiers in conquering the barbarians.

As early as Augustine, the Holy Spirit was associated with bringing life to the world making the Word different than the law. Even though God gave the law, the life-giving Spirit is the one responsible for writing it in the believer's heart. Augustine also spoke of the role of the Spirit in the incarnation; however, he never expected a supernatural manifestation of the Spirit, because the institutional church regulated the life in the Spirit.[21]

During the Reformation, Luther acts as conservative in relation to his colleague Andreas von Carlstadt. During Luther's retreat, after refusing to recant his faith, Carlstadt took charge of the reformation party in Wittenberg. He thought that churches, large or small, were to see by themselves how to act, without any official's intervention, except, the voice of the Spirit under the authority of the Bible, as it was with the first apostles. However, Luther considered this as "a recipe for chaos".[22]

It is unfair to treat the Christendom Paradigm as completely opposed to the work of the Holy Spirit. That is not the case here. The point is that instead of considering the power of the Holy Spirit to further the mission of the church through the spiritual gifts and the believer's disposition to be an agent in the hands of the Holy Spirit, pneumatology during Christendom has been only a doctrine to be studied, not practiced in its entirety. However the Holy Spirit is not seen as a person with whom believers can associate to further the expansion of the kingdom of God continuing Jesus' mission.

Some charismatic movements developed during Christendom. Such movements like the Donatists, who "perpetuated the pneumatic tradition" and thought that the office of the bishop should be in the hands of

---

20. Bosch, *Transforming Mission*, 201.

21. Bromiley, *Historical Theology*, 112, 119; Deiros and Mraida, *Latinoamérica en Llamas*, 30.

22. Placher, *A History of Christian Theology*, 186; Deiros and Mraida, *Latinoamérica en Llamas*, 35.

persons gifted by the Spirit, and demonstrated by their blameless life.[23] The Montanist movement strongly emphasized the gifts of the Spirit for all believers with special emphasis on the gift of prophecy.[24]

Christendom saw also the development of other movements such as the Anabaptist movement of the sixteenth century, which had an apocalyptic vision and the manifestation of the gifts of the Spirit, such as speaking in tongues. In the Methodist Revival different manifestations were attributed to the work of the Spirit such as people screaming, men and women of different ages falling to the floor under the influence of the Spirit, trembling and dancing as praise and worship to God. In the eighteenth century, revivals came under Jonathan Edwards; the nineteenth century was marked by revivals with Charles Finney, Charles Spurgeon and Dwight L. Moody; and in the twentieth century there were the Wales revival, the Pentecostal revival, and the Charismatic revival of the 1960s and 1970s.

Deiros and Mraida give several reasons why the exercising of the gifts of the Spirit ended in western Christianity, around AD 400. They say, because the supernatural gifts found their refuge in the monasteries, the institutionalization of the Spirit in the Church, the nominalism of the believers after the conversion of Constantine robing Christianity of the spiritual power, the regulation of the action of the Spirit by the clergy, and of course, the moral and spiritual decadence of the Church that was, an still is in many instances, more interested in human power than the work of the Spirit.[25]

ESCHATOLOGY IN THE CHRISTENDOM PARADIGM

An important role in defining the last things is how the church views herself. The Augustinian view of the church as equal to the kingdom of God loses the eschatological idea of the coming kingdom.

Throughout Christendom the focus moved from the resurrection to the crucifixion; and the resurrection of Jesus "can only be understood within the framework of prophetic and apocalyptic expectation." It is in Jesus' resurrection that God inaugurates his eschatological purposes for humanity. However, this changes in the following centuries within

---

23. Hägglund, *History of Theology*, 125.
24. Ibid., 57; Deiros and Mraida, *Latinoamérica en Llamas*, 26–28.
25. Deiros and Mraida, *Latinoamérica en Llamas*, 31.

Christendom, especially with regards to the delay of the *paroussia*, which will in turn have a catastrophic effect on the mission of the church.[26]

In Christendom the notion of the first-fruits (1 Cor 15:20, 23; 1 Thess 4:15–17) of the resurrection does not have to do with the eschatological event of the resurrection, because the kingdom of God is already consummated. Therefore, faith is not on the resurrection of Christ followed by all believers, but on the already consummated kingdom. Being in the church is equal to be in the kingdom.[27]

Origen of Alexandria began the allegorization of Scriptures, which took its toll on eschatology. Origen's view of Scriptures was that of a spiritual meaning on the "background of every passage," and if the literal meaning was difficult to extract, "one must hold strictly to the spiritual."[28] By the nineteenth century this type of interpretation would see its effects in the "form criticism" doubting the historicity of Scriptures. However, the historicity of Jesus would suffer the most, having a tremendous effect on eschatology. The theology of Albert Schweitzer, who said that Jesus considered the end of all things at hand and that he was to announce the kingdom, not to found it, impacted eschatology. When God failed to intervene in establishing the kingdom, the early church had to reconstruct its eschatology to reflect the ending of time.[29]

The proclamation of the message of the NT suffered with the eschatology of failure of Schweitzer, when the expectations of the coming of the kingdom were not fulfilled. He emphasized that the message of Jesus was not for modern times, because it belonged to an apocalyptic period different from ours.[30] This developed into a "realized eschatology," that the kingdom of God is already here. Therefore, there is no need to reach others with the gospel message of salvation because the important thing in Christendom is to belong to the church, and since the church is equal with the kingdom, once in the church one is save. The eschatological expectation of the consummation of the kingdom with the coming of the King is lost.

26. Bosch, *Transforming Mission*, 196.
27. Ibid.
28. Hägglund, *History of Theology*, 61–65.
29. Latourette, *Historia del Cristianismo*, Vol. 2, 824; Bosch, *Transforming Mission*, 197.
30. Hägglund, *History of Theology*, 395.

Other important developments of Christendom are post-reformation theology of Calvinism and Arminianism. John Calvin believed in a double predestination of people. Some people were predestined to salvation and others to eternal damnation, because no one can be outside God's dominion. This of course was the seminal seed for strict Calvinism; and its terrible effects on the mission of the church are somewhat obvious. Arminianism, on the other hand, rejects the election concept of the strict Calvinism—that of double predestination as well as irresistible grace and the perseverance of the saints.[31]

With respect to eschatology, both theological perspectives have influenced the mission of the church. Some people adhering to strict Calvinism don't see the need to reach others with the message of salvation, because if they are part of the elect they will come to church. Mission for this view is considered from a social perspective only. There is no eschatological drive that motivates believers to take the message. Arminianism on the other hand, moves believers to reach others with the message of salvation. No one knows who is saved until they have accepted Jesus Christ as Lord in their lives. God's grace is for everyone, whether they believe or not.

Other developments that affected the mission of the church with respect to eschatology may be the rejection of eternal damnation. Eternal damnation is replaced by the idea of universal restoration. Damnation is against the Christian feeling, and universal restoration is "accomplished by the power of salvation."[32] Of course, this kind of eschatology also has to do with the view of a realized eschatology. Everything that needed to be accomplished was done by Christ in his crucifixion; the kingdom has come and been established.

In Christendom, eschatology has become only another aspect of theological studies. The king is only a spiritual figure with whom people have to do, except learn good ethics for present behavior.

MISSIOLOGY IN THE CHRISTENDOM PARADIGM

The concept of the church during Christendom also affected the church's understanding of mission. Since in Christendom the church became one

---

31. Ibid., 268–69; see also Latourette, *Historia del Cristianismo*, Vol. 2, 105, 115; Grenz, *Theology for the Community of God*, 585–88.

32. Hägglund, *History of Theology*, 358.

with the Empire, mission also took a different look. Missionary boundaries were redefined; in Christendom the mission frontier was no longer the neighborhood, as it was the case of the Apostolic Paradigm. Being a citizen of the empire was equal to being a member of the institutional church. There were no boundaries or differences between the world and the church, therefore the missionary frontier disappeared from being at the church's doorstep to the political border of the Empire.[33]

Christendom also experienced a change in the concept of the missionary. The missionary was no longer the regular Christian who took the gospel in his or her going about life, but it became the job of the soldier of the empire and of the professional minister.[34]

Mission during Christendom became equal to conquering other nations. The mission of the church was the "Christianization" of all people instead of being the proclamation of new life in Christ (Matt 28:19). The conqueror was the empire, as opposed to Christ the resurrected Lord who conquered all evil and freed people from the bondage of the law and of the sinful nature.[35]

Christendom is highly marked by the strengthening of structures and the definition of dogmas. The most natural thing to do was to train leaders of the church in how to defend their faith and theology; therefore the order of the day was to make theologians of every person.

Universities emerged during Christendom because of the emergence of urban centers, and the need of a different kind of studies than monasteries. Originally, universities were not centers of higher education as they are in today's world, but they were unions of students and professors, which function was to defend the common interests of all and to certify the degree of preparation of each person.[36]

In order to receive theological education, people were required to go through a process that went from entering the School of Arts to final graduation—sixteen years. Training of the people of God for mission was a long and tedious process, which of course, had its toll on the mission of the church. The loss of identity of mission was the result, since the empire and the church were the same. People during Christendom

33. Mead, *The Once and Future Church*, 14.

34. Ibid.

35. Ibid., Regele, *Death of the Church*, 190; Latourette, *Historia del Cristianismo, Vol. 1*, 139.

36. González, *Historia del Cristianismo, Vol. 1*, 429.

did not need preaching for conversion and salvation, but for instruction. It is the same now.[37]

Leaders from this paradigm considered that only those who graduated from theological institutions were capable of successfully accomplishing the mission. The clergy became a symbol of the sacred and the dispensers of the ministry to the ignorant people. Clergy were the only ones with exclusive access to the mystery of God and to the supernatural gifts of the Spirit. Pastors of this paradigm considered themselves as the chaplains of the community, caring for those who "belong" to the congregation. Since they had the education and were professionals with training, they were the only ones able to adequately care for people.[38]

The role of the Christian was only that of being a good citizen of the empire, and was supposed to support the empire in all of its efforts to "Christianize" all peoples who lived outside the borders of the empire. In the church, believers needed to support their pastors and be receptors of the benefits they provided as sole dispensers of the ministry. In Christendom the responsibility for mission was in the hands of the empire and no longer the church or the believer. In relation to the church in the Christendom paradigm, mission was and still is in the hands of those in leadership of the church, the professional minister.[39]

In Christendom paradigm mission changed from being "centrifugal" to being "centripetal." The centrifugal concept of mission is that of the people of God going to all nations taking the good news of the resurrection of Christ supported by, and in the power of, the Holy Spirit. This includes the going out, becoming part of, proclaiming in the midst of, and being received by. Centripetal concept, on the other hand, is the inward looking state. This includes gathering, inviting, embracing other people, and receiving. The difference in both concepts of mission has to do with the direction of the mission; where is the aim of the force, the intention of those carrying the mission, and the center of the mission, those on the outside, or those in the inside.[40]

---

37. Ibid., 430.

38. Mead, *The Once and Future Church*, 21; Deiros, "The Roots and Fruits of the Argentine Revival," 47–48.

39. Mead, *The Once and Future Church*, 14; Deiros, "The Roots and Fruits of the Argentine Revival," 48.

40. Van Engen, "Biblical Foundations of Mission," 92.2.

When the church is in the centripetal mode, the problem is that it forgets its original mission of going to all nations. In this mode, the church becomes self-centered. The purpose is that of being holy and separated from the world. On the other hand, being only centrifugal, the church fulfills its mission of going out; however, the problem here is that it may become too much like other nations, being no different than them. Nevertheless, when the church is in mission, and is at the same time centripetal and centrifugal, then the church is the salt of the earth and the light of the world (Matt 5:13–16).

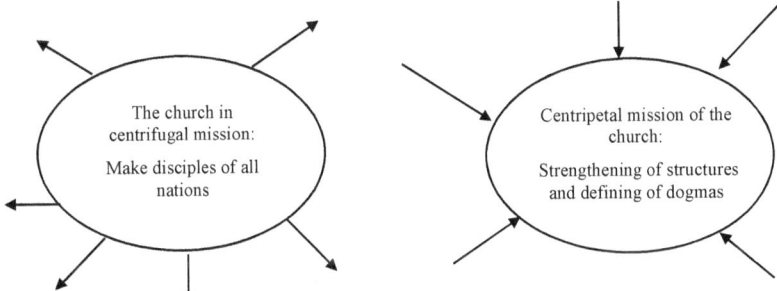

Figure 4. Centripetal and Centrifugal Mission of the Church

The Christendom Paradigm is still in effect in today's church. However, Christendom is not present as the joining of church and state, but in the image of denominations. Denominations have their own boundaries of outreach as well as the missionary enterprises in charge of taking the mission "over there"—mission that was to be understood as to take "democracy" where mission was needed. Clergy are supposed to be loyal to their denomination, as was the case with the empire, where people needed to be loyal to the empire. People in the church are not supposed to do missionary work; that is the role of the professional. Laity is only to support financially, morally, and spiritually by praying for their denominational missionaries.[41]

The Christendom paradigm is seen in the structures that shape traditional denominational churches and other religious institutions that are part of the religious life. Of course the Christendom that survives to the present is not the same one of the medieval times, but one that began to flourish in the nineteen and early twentieth century. The "relics of Christendom," as Mead calls them, is what haunts the church of today

---

41. Regele, *Death of the Church*, 188–89.

and holds her in the past, preventing her from a change.[42] The structural change is what the Christendom paradigm fears, but this is the next stage, a paradigm shift of structures, the New Apostolic Paradigm.

---

42. Mead, *The Once and Future Church*, 18.

4

The New Apostolic Paradigm

CHANGES FROM ONE PARADIGM to another throughout Christianity are difficult to notice. There is not an exact date in the history of the church that marks exactly the shift from one paradigm to the other, because there is also an overlapping time, the time of transition. In exploring this transition then, the main purpose of this chapter is to describe the new and emerging paradigm with respect to its renewed theology and practice of mission.

When questions about basic assumptions of people's worldview begin to emerge, the change process begins. Paradigms begin to shift when people change from one cultural perspective to another, living under a new definition of the boundaries set by the new worldview. This causes anomalies in how one act according to the present paradigm, finding difficult or failing in accomplishing any results according to the paradigm in the present.[1]

This is exactly what is happening with the Christendom Paradigm. The present paradigm is not functioning well, especially for today's generation of Christians, not only considering age, but the way people perceive Christianity. Christianity is becoming irrelevant for many, not because of Christianity itself, but because the rules and regulations set by the Christendom Paradigm make it difficult, and in most cases, fail to accomplish the mission of the church.

---

1. Regele, *Death of the Church*, 192.

UNDERSTANDING THE NAME "NEW APOSTOLIC PARADIGM"

The change from modernity to postmodernity has also influenced the paradigm shift. Theological assumptions based on modernity are becoming irrelevant, and consumerism, a byproduct of modernity, is coming to light. Local congregations willing to live by God's rules will overcome consumerism, becoming "alternative communities" and providing shelter for those escaping Christendom as we know it.[2]

A new paradigm emerges when the church's understanding of being the church and of its mission changes.[3] However, the fear of change, leaving the comfort zone, is the reason why the new paradigm has not been recognized. It is the fear of something new not knowing how to handle it, that makes people avoid the subject. Nevertheless, it is nothing new only renewed.

Mead calls this time "the time between paradigms."[4] Regele calls it "paradigm in flux."[5] Whatever the terminology, this points to the time between paradigms, an ambiguous time for many, thus calling it "liminality," a term describing the transition process accompanying a change of state or social position.[6]

However difficult to assimilate the change, one thing is true: that the church of the present is changing its understanding of being the church and of its mission. This will inevitably lead to a new paradigm, which at this time is emerging, and in some places is already in place.

Elmer Towns points to the fact that "we live in changing times," and that new congregations begin to emerge as old ones die;[7] we also see new evangelistic methods of church growth as old ones become irrelevant due to cultural irrelevancy, as well as the emerging of new forms of expressing worship in order to be relevant to society. This is the time of the local congregation; the time of going back and living up to the New Testament roots, in order to accomplish the church's mission.[8]

---

2. Vallet and Zech, *The Mainline Church's Funding Crisis*, 139–41.
3. Mead, *The Once and Future Church*.
4. Ibid., 22.
5. Regele, *Death of the Church*, 191.
6. Roxburgh, *The Missionary Congregation, Leadership and Liminality*, 23–24; Vallet and Zech, *The Mainline Church's Funding Crisis*, 140.
7. Towns, "Foreword," 7–9.
8. Towns, *Is the Day of the Denomination Dead?*, 13.

The naming of the present state of the church has been the subject of controversy. Wagner, a pioneer in discovering this pattern in the church, has had difficulty in naming it, coming up with a list of names such as postdenominationalism, independent charismatic, interdependent charismatic, and finally settling for "new apostolic reformation."[9]

However, Wagner's name implies a movement,[10] such as was the case of the Methodists or the Lutherans that ended up in becoming denominations. This is not the case of the New Apostolic Paradigm (NAP). As I mentioned in chapter 1, I use the term paradigm to describe an epoch of the church's history. In this regard, a paradigm marks a period of time of the church in mission. Therefore, in the NAP there is a new way of understanding the church and mission, thus, the NAP is not a movement leading to a denomination, like the ones mentioned above.

Why the name New Apostolic Paradigm? Because the focus is not on denominations as such, but in this paradigm the focus and agent of mission is the local congregation. It is a church that comes out of the New Testament, with a vision and burden for the lost; one that feeds its members with the purpose of involving them in mission; one that not only provides assurance of salvation, but also practical insights for daily life; one that even being small in size has the vision to grow and accomplish the Great Commission. These are local congregations that identify themselves not by their denominational affiliation, but by their own trademark, logo, and ministry. The emphasis is in the new life offered by the resurrection of Christ, rather than membership of the church.[11]

It is "new" in the sense that it points to the new understanding of being the church, as opposed to the "old," pointing out to the Christendom Paradigm. However, "new" is also intended to show the distinction from the Apostolic Paradigm in name, but also the similarities with it. "New

---

9. Wagner, "The New Apostolic Reformation," 13–25; see also Wagner, *Churchquake*, 38–43.

10. The implication of movement has to do with the view of the Methodist or Lutherans for example. They began as a movement and became denominations. This is not to say that Wagner is considering the New Apostolic Reformation as the formation of a new denomination; on the contrary, he considers the New Apostolic Reformation as an "extraordinary work of God . . . changing the shape of Protestant Christianity around the world." It is therefore, a movement initiated by God, and not by human beings (Wagner, *Churchquake*, 5).

11. Towns, *Is the Day of the Denomination Dead?*, 131–36; Easum, *Dancing With Dinosaurs*, 42.

Apostolic" is also a distinction from other churches that adopted the term "apostolic" but that operate under the Christendom Paradigm.[12]

"Apostolic," on the other hand, points out to the new understanding of being the church. Van Engen says that when local congregations "see themselves as branch offices of the kingdom of God" they will closely examine their roll in fulfilling Jesus' mission. He goes on to say "the role of the local church in the world involves the church in an apostolate received from, guided by, and patterned after the mission of Jesus." This is the "transferred apostolate."[13]

Furthermore, the endowment of the gifts of the Spirit upon the people of God compels the people of God to continue the mission of Jesus in a similar way as He did. Signs and wonders follow the preaching of the Word, and the exercising of the office of prophet, priest, and king, as related to Jesus' role in ministry, are the expression of the transferred apostolate.[14] This transferred apostolate has given way to an apostolic spirit sweeping local congregations. This is a sense of being sent by God to make disciples of all nations, to free the captives, open the eyes of the blind, and to proclaim the good will of the Lord (see Luke 4:18–19).

People within the new paradigm are called apostolic people, those with an apostolic spirit who earnestly work toward reaching people for God, planting and multiplying churches. Churches with the apostolic spirit are also considered as apostolic churches, some call them "churches of the new paradigm,"[15] or "paradigm communities."[16] These are congregations that have a different understanding of what is being the church. Also, the 1980s and 1990s gave way to the emergence and wide recognition of the restoration of the office and ministry of the prophet and apostle, and the rapid multiplication of apostolic networks has given way to name the present state as "new apostolic paradigm."[17]

New Apostolic Paradigm does not name a movement, as previously said. New Apostolic Paradigm is a way to designate the present period

---

12. Wagner, *Churchquake*, 37.

13. Engen, *God's Missionary People*, 119.

14. Ibid., 120–22.

15. Miller, *Reinventing American Protestantism*, 1.

16. Easum, *Dancing With Dinosaurs*, 57.

17. Cannistraci, *Apostles and the Emerging Apostolic Movement*, 24–25; Deiros, *Protestantismo en América Latina: Ayer, Hoy y Mañana*, 92; Wagner, "Revival Power," 16; *Churchquake*, 46.

of the church in mission that resembles more and more the pattern of the Apostolic Paradigm. Similarities with the Apostolic Paradigm are in the way Christianity is lived out, not only studied; the church is seen as a charismatic community; the understanding of the need to rely on the *dunamis* of God to effectively fulfill the mission; the eschatological drive to fulfill the mission because Christ is coming in the near future, probably within the present generation; and, of course, the restoration of the ministry of prophet and apostle, which in combination with the evangelist and pastor-teacher will guide the church to its unity and maturity.[18]

CHRISTOLOGY IN THE NEW APOSTOLIC PARADIGM

One important characteristic of the NAP is its Christology. During the Christendom Paradigm emphasis was in the search for a historical Jesus as a result of the many heresies about Jesus' humanity. However, the strong emphasis on the Jesus of the cross as means to develop a theology of salvation and justification by faith also jeopardizes the Jesus of the resurrection.

The church during Christendom devoted its life to worshipping the Jesus of the cross, remembering his death. Instead of celebrating Jesus' resurrection, Christendom Paradigm remembered Jesus' crucifixion. This put a strong emphasis on a "docetic"[19] Christ, as oppose to an incarnational one, the living Christ who dwells in and among his people.[20]

In the NAP, a strong emphasis is put on the church as an organism, as opposed to an institutionalized organization.[21] This concept of the church as an organism can only be conceived of by an incarnational Christology; that is, a Christ who is the life-giving source for the organism called church.[22]

In similar manner, the incarnational Christ calls for a change of attitude in the life of the believer and the church as well. A change from orthodoxy to orthopraxis, which Pablo Deiros calls "a praxiological

---

18. Wagner, *Churchquake*, 44–46; Mead, *The Once and Future Church*, 24–25; Cannistraci, *Apostles and the Emerging Apostolic Movement*, 21–44.

19. By docetic I don't mean the heretic view confronted during the Apostolic Paradigm, but docetic as opposed to real, the resurrected and ever present Christ among the worshiping community who is the Head of the church and the source of its life.

20. Ogden, *The New Reformation*, 45.

21. See the section of this document dealing with ecclesiology in the New Apostolic Paradigm.

22. Ibid., 33.

revolution," faith in action expressed in the conduct of the believer in the world. This change has to do with the understanding and practicing of the Lordship of Christ. There is no distinction between Christ the Savior and Christ the Lord. "Salvation is not a past experience anymore, but an ever present one, expressed in a continuous commitment to the Lord."[23] Christ is Lord and God, and a personal relationship with Jesus Christ means the difference between heaven and hell.[24]

This is the incarnational Christ of the NAP, a vivid reality of the Lordship of Christ. The fruit of this vivid reality is a different understanding of salvation, a vivid discipleship and obedience to the Lord. This is also in tune with the *Missio Dei* concept, because it is a community of *praxis*, which in obedience to the Lord understands its position as the body of Christ, the instrument of God's mission now sent into the world.[25]

This kind of incarnational Christology brings out the closeness of God to his people. The people of God realize that the Christ of the resurrection is not only involved in religious affairs, but he is also involved in human affairs. That is, a Christ who understands the sufferings of his people, the oppression of the poor and the weak, and the loneliness of the social outcast. As Pablo Deiros puts it, the closer that God is to people in their everyday life, the easier it will be for them to act on his behalf. The less docetic Christ is, the easier to commit to him in every aspect of life, including "the fight for justice, truth, peace, and liberty."[26]

Because this is a living Christ, the life-giver and sustainer of the church as an organism, he is always in touch with this people. Thus, the people of God are "sacramental people," the means of grace and the bearers of the presence of Christ, and the church becomes "the container, and Jesus the one who fills it with his life."[27]

In the concept of the church as an organism, the body of Christ, Jesus is the Head of the church, as opposed to the professional minister, the bishop or vicar (whatever the title may be) in the Christendom Paradigm. Believers in the NAP draw their life from Christ, who leads the church. They are absolutely dependent on Christ.

---

23. Deiros, *Protestantismo en América*, 108–10. Translation is mine.

24. Wagner, *Churchquake*, 67.

25. Deiros, *Protestantismo en América Latina*, 127; Bosch, *Transforming Mission*, 390–91.

26. Deiros, *Protestantismo en América Latina*, 128.

27. Ogden, *The New Reformation*, 31.

Even though pastors lead large congregations in the NAP, they still submit to the authority of Christ. Pastors of the new paradigm churches ask Christ, as the Head of the church, where "he thinks the church should go" and expect in prayer an answer.[28] Christ is then the Head of the church and ultimate authority. The people of God obediently submit to the Head, because they are the body of Christ, fulfilling the role assigned to each one by the Spirit.[29]

As the Head of the church, Christ is also seen as the Chief Apostle. He is the one sent by God with a redemptive mission and as Head of the apostolic people, the church. Christ is also the one who sends his people to continue his mission. Thus the church becomes apostolic in nature.[30]

However, Christ is not only considered as the Head of the church, but he is also the foundation. As the life-giver Christ, he is also the sustainer and the equipper of the church. The people of God draw life from the indwelling presence of Christ, but are also sustained by Christ. As the Head, each member is directly connected to him who gives life as well as direction. Only when Christ is the Head and the foundation, can the church truly accomplish its purpose of bringing glory to God in worship, community, and witness.[31]

PNEUMATOLOGY IN THE NEW APOSTOLIC PARADIGM

One of the main characteristics of the Christendom Paradigm is the fact that the church was identified with the Empire. For this reason, everybody living within the limits of the Empire was considered as a Christian. Mission was to be conducted by the Empire, and the power needed for mission was military.

The Christendom Paradigm has only studied Pneumatology as a doctrine. The Holy Spirit was not seen as a person with whom believers could have an active and personal relationship, and who endowed believers with the *dunamis* of God for effectiveness in accomplishing the mission.

This is not the case of the NAP. The NAP is highly marked by its closeness with the Holy Spirit, not as doctrine, but as an active helper who

---

28. Wagner, *Churchquake*, 86–87.

29. Ogden, *The New Reformation*, 35.

30. Cannistraci, *Apostles and the Emerging Apostolic Movement*, 57, 59; Van Engen, *God's Missionary People*, 119–20.

31. Ogden, *The New Reformation*, 108–9; Snyder, *Radical Renewal*, 118–19.

endows believers in the mission of God. The three main characteristics of the pneumatology of the New Apostolic Paradigm are: a generalization of a Holy Spirit experience, an awakening of the gifts of the Spirit, and a manifestation of the power of God.

A Generalization of a Holy Spirit Experience

The history of the church gives evidence of several times when a tremendous outpouring of the Holy Spirit characterized the church of the time. Many times those who experienced a different manifestation than traditional Christianity were considered as strange, if not heretic. However, in the twentieth century, a more generic term began to identify those who had a Holy Spirit experience; they came to be known as "Pentecostals" because of their Pentecost-like experience of Acts 2:4.[32]

The earliest form of Pentecostalism in the first half of the twentieth century was usually associated with the lower socioeconomic classes. Nevertheless, a hunger for renewal moved the historic and affluent denominations, which resulted in several spiritual manifestations, such as healings, speaking in tongues and the exercising of the gifts of the Spirit by all believers. By 1960, the Charismatic movement reaching historic and affluent denominations became noticeable by the ministry of Dennis Bennett, an Episcopal Rector in Van Nuys, California. Roots of the Charismatic movement can be traced as far back as the 1940s. With the help of divine healing evangelist such as William Barnham, Oral Roberts, Gordon Lindsay, and T. L. Osborne, the "Spirit-filled Life" Christianity beyond the traditional Pentecostalism gained popularity.[33]

In the 1980s, another outpouring of the Holy Spirit upon the historic denominational churches took place. This outpouring of the Holy Spirit became known as the "Third Wave" when Wagner coined the name in 1983. The Third Wave is considered as the successor of the Pentecostal movement (First Wave), and the Charismatic movement (Second Wave).

This new wave of the Holy Spirit is comprised of those evangelicals belonging to traditional denominations that experience the power of the Holy Spirit, speak in other tongues, and exercise other gifts of the Sprit

---

32. Deiros and Mraida, *Latinoamérica en Llamas*, 37–44; Burgess, et al., "The Pentecostal and Charismatic Movements," 1–2.

33. Burgess, et al., "The Pentecostal and Charismatic Movements," 3–4; Hocken, "Charismatic Movement," 130–60.

such as casting out demons and prophecy. However, they don't want to label themselves as Charismatic or Pentecostals. Important characteristics of the Third Wave are: the belief in the baptism of the Holy Spirit at conversion which is different from a second blessing; several fillings with the Spirit subsequent to the original baptism; ministry under the anointing of the Holy Spirit by all believers rather than one individual; and the compromise in different areas such as raising up of hands and speaking in tongues in public worship in order to avoid divisions.[34]

What we can see, especially with the last two waves of the Holy Spirit outpouring, is a generalization of the Holy Spirit experience. The NAP, which in some way originates from the Second and Third Waves, is highly marked by what Deiros calls "a growing 'Pentecostalization' of the Christian experience in general." Believers of the NAP try to live out their faith in a "supernatural dimension under the Lordship of Christ." This new reality is going from a historic Protestantism to a more Pentecostal—charismatic one.[35]

Another important aspect of pneumatology in the NAP is the concept of the anointing. As previously mentioned, the "Pentecostalization" of Christianity is giving way to a generalized experience with the Holy Spirit. This in turn calls for new theological terms that describe a person's experience of the fullness of the Spirit.

The anointing is a term that describes "the experience of the fullness of the Holy Spirit, in ways that are more or less in accord with standard evangelical teaching on the subject."[36] As previously mentioned, one of the characteristics of the Third Wave is belief in the baptism of the Holy Spirit at conversion with subsequent fillings. Pentecostals, on the other hand, consider the Spirit baptism as subsequent to salvation, a "once and for all" gift. The anointing then comes as a "compromise term" to identify the experience of the fullness of the Spirit in a believer's life.

Manifestations of the anointing are similar to the Pentecostal-Charismatic experience. Speaking in tongues, crying, laughter, and falling down under the power of the Spirit are characteristics of the anointing. The anointing gained popularity in the 1990s with the publication of the

---

34. Wagner, "Third Wave," 844–45; Deiros, "The Roots and Fruits of the Argentine Revival," 33–34.

35. Deiros, "The Roots and Fruits of the Argentine Revival," 34; *Protestantismo en América Latin*, 120–22.

36. Deiros, "The Roots and Fruits of the Argentine Revival," 39.

books *The Anointing* and *Good Morning Holy Spirit* by Charismatic pastor Benny Hinn of the Orlando Christian Center in Florida. In Argentina, Claudio Freidzon popularized the anointing after a visit to Hinn, and during the last part of 1992 and the beginnings of 1993 the anointing renewed many evangelical churches. Being a characteristic of believers in the NAP, the anointing fills people with enthusiasm and zeal for the mission of God in reaching others with the gospel.[37]

The baptism of the Holy Spirit is considered by the Pentecostal tradition as subsequent to salvation. Because the emphasis is on the once-and-for all experience, this can be considered as an assurance for salvation. The anointing on the other hand, although it is a Holy Spirit experience, emphasizes the fullness of the Spirit to live a more active and productive Christian life. Many historic-denominational believers, who for the most part are Calvinist in their theology, don't experience the anointing as assurance of salvation, but as a life of continual renewal in the power of the Spirit.

An Awakening of the Gifts of the Spirit

With respect to the gifts of the Spirit, during the Christendom Paradigm, they became exclusive of the clergy. The Holy Spirit was institutionalized, and in the early beginnings of Christendom, supernatural gifts found refuge in the monastery. Clergy was solely capable of prophesying, of evangelizing, of counseling, and of exercising pastoral care for the congregation.[38]

The NAP on the other hand is characterized by an awakening of the gifts of the Spirit. It is an awakening, not only in the desire to study about the gifts of the Spirit, but to actively practice them by all believers. The ministry of all believers is an important aspect of the NAP, where a democratization of the *charismata* is occurring, returning the spiritual gifts to the body of Christ. This brings a biblical unity among the members of the body, which in combination with the governmental gifts of Eph 4:11, produces, the growth of the church.[39]

---

37. Ibid., 39–41; Easum, *Dancing With Dinosaurs*, 40, 42, 47; Bruner, *A Theology of the Holy Spirit*, 38–39; 82–84.

38. Deiros and Mraida, *Latinoamérica en Llamas*, 31; Deiros, "The Roots and Fruits of the Argentine Revival," 48.

39. Ibid., 50; Wagner, "Third Wave," 15.

The church in the NAP is shifting from being an institutionalized organization to a living organism as the body of Christ. When the church is seen in the organic model, every member shares the experience of the Spirit; and the continuous manifestation of the spiritual gifts is what constitutes the "life and growth of the community as the body of Christ." Therefore, the gifts of the Spirit are essential for the living organism to be called the church. Even though gifts are for individuals, they are for the welfare of the community, and "Christian community exists only in the living interplay of charismatic ministry, in the actual being and doing for others in words and deeds."[40]

Howard Snyder[41] in his understanding of the ecology of the church considers the small group or cell group as the best environment for the church to accomplish its mission. David Finell[42] also considers the cell group as vital to the body of Christ. However, he goes beyond in saying that in cell groups, people can exercise their spiritual gifts in order to accomplish God's mission. Bob Logan[43] considers that mobilizing believers according to their spiritual gifts brings growth to the church. This shows how vital the gifts of the Spirit are in the church, which is the understanding in the NAP.

Nevertheless, the most prominent aspect of the awakening of the gifts of the Spirit in the NAP is the restoring of the "gift and office of prophet" in the 1980s. The decade of the 1980s has been marked by the emergence of this gift, as well as the renewal of other spiritual gifts. The gift of prophecy, from the 1980s on, is no longer understood as exhortation, edification, and the exposition of the Word of God only, but also as a more direct, specific, and guiding kind of prophecy, as in the New Testament times.[44]

The 1990s saw the restoration of the office and ministry of the apostle. With the restoration of the ministry and office of the apostle, came the emergence of apostolic networks,[45] rapidly spreading throughout

---

40. Dunn, "Models of Christian Community in the New Testament," 6; Snyder, *Radical Renewal*, 139.

41. Snyder, *Radical Renewal*.

42. Finell, *Life in His Body*.

43. Logan, *Beyond Church Growth*.

44. Wagner, "The New Apostolic Reformation," 16; Deiros, *Protestantismo en América Latina*, 91.

45. An explanation of what apostolic networks are is given in the section dealing with

Christianity, giving way to appropriately calling this period of time a New Apostolic Paradigm.[46]

The practice of the gifts of the Spirit in the NAP is not only that of commonly accepted concepts of the Pentecostal and Charismatic movements. The inclusion of the government gifts of apostle, prophet, evangelist, and pastor-teacher is also widely accepted. However, the apostle and prophet ministries concept is different.

A Manifestation of the Power of God

As was the case of the Apostolic Paradigm, the Holy Spirit is also the *dunamis* of God in the NAP. As with the restoration of the office and ministries of apostle and prophet, the 1980s and 1990s saw the emergence of the spiritual warfare movement. Spiritual warfare requires the dynamic power of God in the life of the believer. Wagner notes that in previous decades a vocabulary containing such terms as "strategic level spiritual warfare, spiritual mapping, identificational repentance, and prayer evangelism" were not part of the Christian vocabulary.[47]

In the NAP, signs and wonders are characteristic of producing massive conversions as a result of the dynamic power of God through the Holy Spirit. In Latin America, several evangelistic ministries have emerged with a strong emphasis on divine healing and liberation from demonic oppression and possession.[48]

Power evangelism is also characteristic of the NAP. This concept follows the idea that signs and wonders must follow the proclamation of the gospel to authenticate the message. Besides, the objective is not only the conversion of people, but also the deliverance from the devil. Power evangelism goes beyond allegiance and truth encounters. Allegiance encounter is only a change of commitment, and truth encounter is about understanding—a realization of what one is living is wrong. However, truth and allegiance encounters produce nominal Christians, whereas

---

ecclesiology in the New Apostolic Paradigm.

46. Wagner, "Revival Power," 16; Deiros, *Protestantismo en América Latina*, 92.

47. Wagner, "Revival Power: God Has Set His People 'A-Praying,'" 16–17.

48. Deiros, *Protestantismo en América Latina*, 92; Deiros and Mraida, *Latinoamérica en Llamas*, 125.

power encounter is a confrontation with the power of God. People then know God not only in the Word, but also by experience.[49]

The Holy Spirit in the NAP is not only a person who Christians believe in, but He is usually invited to fellowship with believers. Fellowship with the Holy Spirit comes in worship, with contemporary music and the manifestations of healings, deliverance from demonic oppression, intercessory prayer, which opens the way to the preaching of the Word.[50]

ECCLESIOLOGY IN THE NEW APOSTOLIC PARADIGM

When one begins to question basic assumptions, the change process begins, culminating in a new worldview. This is the case of the concept of the church during Christendom, which began with the reformers questioning, among other things, the common believer's role.

Priesthood of All Believers

With respect to the priesthood of all believers, it comes to mind that Martin Luther's strong emphasis sent a shock wave that made the institutional church tremble. However, the concept of the priesthood of all believers has not been completely applied to this date. This concept considers that all believers have access to scriptures, the ability to interpret scriptures, access to God through Christ, which implies salvation and justification by faith, not by becoming a member of the institutional church, among other things.

Nevertheless, the priesthood of all believers goes beyond this concept. Priesthood implies mediation before God and before people. Therefore being a priest is not only gained access to minister to God, but also to minister to each other as members of the body of Christ. Even though this concept is taught, believed, and proclaimed by churches and denominations, it is not practiced by releasing believers into ministry.[51]

In the NAP, the concept is that of the ministry of all the people of God. The concept of the ministry of the laity, as is also known, was the beginning of the change. However, this concept still sees two kinds of people in the church, clergy and laity, which is pretty much in accordance with

---

49. Deiros and Mraida, *Latinoamérica en Llamas*, 128; Kraft, *Anthropology for Christian Witness*, 453.

50. Wagner, "The New Apostolic Reformation," 25.

51. Rainer, *Giant Awakenings*, 92; Ogden, *The New Reformation*, 11–12.

the Christendom Paradigm, which considers two levels of Christianity: "the common people were at the lower level" and those with "the privilege to preside at the altar of the communion."[52]

Mead notes that "ministry of the laity" is a phrase that recognizes the death of the old way of seeing the church in ministry, but at the same time, it is so often used in today's church-world that is has lost its intended meaning.[53] Personally, I prefer "ministry of all the people of God" instead of "ministry of the laity." The first phrase calls for ministry of the church as a body, where every member has a function. The latter one calls for a separation of people within the church.[54]

The priesthood of all believers cannot be totally understood apart from one's concept of the church. The Christendom Paradigm, which prevails in many instances, sees the church as an institution, an institutionalized organization which ministry is "from top down to its official leaders." On the other hand, in the NAP the church is considered as an organism, "a life-pulsating people who are animated by the indwelling presence of Jesus Christ."[55] The church as an organism is an organic community where everyone exists for the other, bringing new life, because of the indwelling presence of Christ, to those dying or already dead in the community's surroundings; even to the point of "spending one's life unto death" for the sake of one's society.[56]

When the church is conceived of as an organism, a living organism made of many members, the church practices the priesthood of all believers and not only teaches about it. The idea is that every member is a minister empowered for the work of the ministry. The keyword here is "empowerment." To empower is different from delegate. To delegate is to give someone a job to do under close supervision to the point of actually telling the person what to do. To empower, on the other hand, is to teach someone how to do a job and for that person to continue doing it without close supervision, but providing reports from time to time, because one has been rightfully equipped to perform that job. However, there still is accountability.

---

52. Rainer, *Giant Awakenings*, 90.
53. Mead, *The Once and Future Church*, 24.
54. Ogden, *The New Reformation*, 65–69.
55. Ibid., 29, 45.
56. Easum, *Dancing With Dinosaurs*, 56.

Wagner notes that pastors in the NAP understand the need of the ministry of all the people of God in order to provide a continuous growth of the congregation.[57] The continuous growth of the congregation is not only numerical, but it is most of all, a healthy growth of the body of Christ, when everyone understands his/her "responsibility as stewards of the gifts and call"[58] of God to do the work of the ministry. However, until the view of the church as an organism is divorced from the "institutional theology of the church,"[59] the practice of the priesthood of all believers will be hindered.

Authority

The understanding of authority in the NAP is greatly affected by the understanding of the church. Because in the Christendom Paradigm the church is viewed as an institution instead of an organism, authority is bureaucratic, positional, rational and institutionally centered. On the other hand, in the NAP authority has a new concept, because the church is seen as an organism. Authority then is personal, relational, charismatic, and democratic.[60]

Personal type of authority is different to that of bureaucratic type. The focus of personal authority is the person itself instead of a bureaucratic type. In this case it is the person who has authority instead of a committee or board. Authority on a personal level is on the basis of trust. Wagner notes that traditionally it is more common to trust a group of people than an individual. Then the key factor in the NAP is trust: "If trust is the root, authority is the fruit."[61] Furthermore, authority is given to a person by the followers based on the "credibility of a leader who is able to deliver on what is promised."[62]

Authority is also relational as opposed to positional or hierarchical. Positional authority comes with the title of what one does, as opposed to who one is. In a positional type of authority people follow and obey because they have to. In this case, the area of influence will not go beyond

---

57. Wagner, *Churchquake*, 210.
58. Ogden, *The New Reformation*, 163.
59. Ibid., 56.
60. Democratic means participatory. Where everybody has something to do, and where the church is the people, not the clergy. See Wagner, "The New Apostolic Reformation," 20.
61. Wagner, *Churchquake*, 81.
62. Gibbs, *ChurchNext*, 75.

one's job description. Because authority is in the title, not in the person, it will create difficulty in working with volunteers. Working with volunteers is a characteristic of the NAP, because being a member of the body of Christ is using the God given gifts for the profit of the whole body.[63]

Relationships are the base for authority instead of enforcing or coercing. In the NAP authority is recognized on the church leader because they, leader and followers, have developed a long-term relationship, which have acted as testimony of the leader's ability. Therefore, authority is conferred.

Leaders in the NAP are servants. Therefore, servanthood is the model out which authority comes from. Leaders have in mind God's mission through them and the church, putting aside any personal agenda to serve God's purposes. For this reason, their goal is to support instead of control, to recognize those who help accomplish the mission instead of shining as lonely stars, to share leadership by not being trapped in the title game, but recognizing Christian character instead of the office or position one holds.[64]

David Cannistraci uses the analogy of fatherhood to illustrate authority in the NAP. This analogy has to do with mentoring others. Even though the generic term he uses is fatherhood, women are not excluded from mentoring others. The role of a mentor in fatherhood is emphasized in the NAP. As a father cares for the growth and welfare of the family, in similar manner leaders of the NAP care for the growth and development of the household of God.[65]

Authority in the NAP is also charismatic, as opposed to rational. The NAP emphasizes the idea of function over operation. Leaders are leaders because of their spiritual gifts and not because of the position. Therefore the spiritual gifts and Christian character one exercises evidence authority. Authority is not in the office and does not come with the title, but is bestowed from on high.[66]

However, when the church acts in an institutionalized way as opposed to a charismatic one, then "spiritual gifts are replaced by aptitude,

---

63. Maxwell, *Desarrolle el Líder que Está en Usted*, 18–20; Wagner, "The New Apostolic Reformation," 20.

64. Cannistraci, *Apostles and the Emerging Apostolic Movement*, 146–47; Ogden, *the New Reformation*, 176–77.

65. Cannistraci, *Apostles and the Emerging Apostolic Movement*, 118.

66. Ogden, *The New Reformation*, 141–42.

education and technique"⁶⁷ then leaders become superstars. When "[a]nointed leaders are replaced by managers"⁶⁸ the maintenance state begins instead of a continuous growth, and authority becomes centered on institutional structure.

Yet, authority in the NAP is also democratic as opposed to institutionally centered. Democratic has to do more with the involvement in ministry of all the people of God, than a form of government. Democratic then is participatory, a church where the people have something to do, and a church that is the people, not the clergy.

When authority is democratic, every member of the church is a member of the body with different ministries. Therefore, leaders are seen as "first-among-equals." Leaders are servants rather than first on the ladder. Everybody has the opportunity to develop his/her ministry call. The leader shares the vision and accepts input from others, then modifies the vision for the benefit of the body. Other members of the staff who are endowed with different gifts are "fully rested with authority to dream and implement a vision."⁶⁹

Cannistraci considers authority in the NAP as based on four principles: "Interdependent cooperation," meaning autonomy of the churches and of the people exercising free will, yet submitting to each other; "voluntary submission," where nobody is coerced, but personal relationships bring about respect and submission; "local autonomy," wherein leaders in the NAP respect each other as leaders of God's flock; and "mutual accountability."⁷⁰ This last principle is important because everybody is accountable to each other.

In the institutionalized way, accountability is from the top down. However, in the NAP where the organic model of the church takes precedence, there is mutual accountability, which "means to have a stake in the success of fellow partners in ministry.⁷¹ Leaders in the NAP are accountable to the people they serve, because their personal agenda is aside, and the focus is the equipping of the saints for the work of the ministry (Eph 4:12).

---

67. Snyder, *Radical Renewal*, 139–40.
68. Ogden, *The New Reformation*, 144.
69. Ibid., 178–81.
70. Cannistraci, *Apostles and the Emerging Apostolic Movement*, 148–52.
71. Ogden, *The New Reformation*, 182.

Restructuring of the Church

In the NAP the church is seeing a restructuring. As previously mentioned, one of the important aspects of the NAP is the practice of the ministry of all believers, by using their God-given gifts. It is basically for this reason that the church is considered more as an organism than as an institutionalized organization.[72]

Snyder develops the concept of the "Ecology of the Church." This is an organic model of the church, a living organism viewed "as a dynamic interplay of many parts." Snyder says that the main purpose of the church is to glorify God according to the basic functions of worship, community and witness.[73] Snyder explores the basic functions by expanding on each of the functions. Worship is viewed as instruction, repentance and celebration; community as discipline, sanctification, and the gifts of the Spirit; and witness as evangelism, service, and justice (Figure 5).

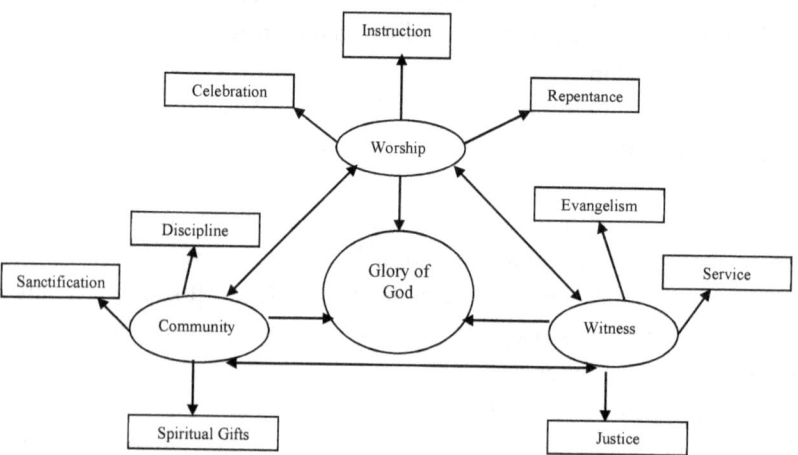

Figure 5. The Ecology of the Church

However, for this model to function, the structure of the church must change. If the church is seen as an organism where every member has a role or "as a dynamic interplay of many parts," then an organic model that fulfills the basic functions of worship, community and witness must replace the hierarchical structure of the institution.

The basic structure of the church in the NAP that fulfills the organic model is the small group. Small groups of 8-16 people meeting regularly

72. Ibid., 45, 54–55; Snyder, *Radical Renewal*, 11.
73. Snyder, *Radical Renewal*, 117–20.

in a house for worship, community and witness. These are the groups that can fulfill the mission of the church in the postmodern world. They are compatible with the organic model of the church, to the point that the generic term to refer to them is "cells."[74]

Cells are the basic building blocks in any form of life. In similar way, cells are considered as the basic building blocks of the body of Christ out of which life springs to the body by natural multiplication.[75] Multiplication in cell groups occur when the members of the group reach other people with the gospel (witness), bring them to the weekly meeting for discipleship, personal ministry and to community (community), and celebrate new life in Christ by singing, exercising spiritual gifts, and ministering to others (worship).

The new structure in the NAP considers cell groups as the church, not as another ministry of the local congregation. The mentality of the church is focused on the "going" instead of "bringing." The church is "in" the community, among the community, as opposed to "out of," outside of, or on the side of the community.[76]

In this kind of structure the people of God have different roles in the body as opposed to rank in a hierarchy. In the Christendom Paradigm, the role of the professionally ordained minister was to care for the congregation and to bring new members to the congregation. The pastor was an important part of the community who brought stability to the entire town.

The pastor was the central figure, the person who organized Sunday worship service, the one who taught the Bible, and preached the message of salvation and grace several times a week if necessary. Professional-ordained ministers are supposed to give while the people receive. Professional-ordained ministers become "omni-competent." They are the center of attention, the ones that can do anything that needs to be done.[77]

However, in the NAP the structure is different. The roles of the leaders and of the people change in the NAP as well. People change from

---

74. Ibid., 149; Comiskey, *Home Cell Group Explosion*, 17–21; Easum, *Dancing With Dinosaurs*, 57–58.

75. Comiskey, *Home Cell Group Explosion*, 19.

76. Easum, *Dancing With Dinosaurs*, 62–63; Comiskey, *Home Cell Group Explosion*, 17; Finell, *Life in His Body*, 13–17.

77. Easum, *Dancing With Dinosaurs*, 58–60; Rainer, *Giant Awakenings*, 105, 108–9.

being passive receivers to active participants and the professional/ordained minister from being active achiever to an active equipper.

Elton Trueblood says that the ministry is for everybody a call to share the life of Christ; but the pastorate only "for those who possess the gifts to help men and women to practice any ministry for which they have been called."[78] This means that the professional ministry is responsible for sharing the knowledge acquired by equipping the saints for the work of the ministry (Eph 4:12).

Therefore, the professional minister, the pastor of the local congregation, becomes equipper of the saints.[79] The pastor's role is that of equipping the people of God for the work of the ministry. As an equipper of saints, the pastor's role is not that of doing the work of the ministry, but that of helping discover the gifts, develop the gifts, and training others for ministry by using their gifts. In doing so, the pastor will build teams of people to share the ministry of the church in worship, community, and witness, decentralizing the ministry from him/herself to the whole people of God. Success then will not be on how much attention the pastor can bring upon him/herself as superstar, but on the "redemptive character that emerges from the congregation and teams."[80]

Greg Ogden notes that hierarchical titles also change in the NAP.[81] Such titles as "senior, associate, and assistant" are changed, because they are representatives of position rather than function. Other titles such as reverend, doctor or minister only represent the status and many times give people the idea that the ministry is for those with the official title only.[82]

Also characteristic of the NAP is the formation of networks; specifically, apostolic networks. Apostolic networks are different from denominations. Denominations are the result of divisions as fruit of the seed of

---

78. Trueblood, *La Iglesia: Un Compañerismo Incendiario*, 36; Ogden, *The New Reformation*, 97.

79. I want to clarify that when I refer to professional minister, I mean each of the government gifts of Ephesians 4:11. This also means that when I refer to the "pastor's" role, I have in mind the Christian leader of a congregation or group, developing his/her ministry as pastor of a church.

80. Trueblood, *La Iglesia: Un Compañerismo Incendiario*, 39; see also Ogden, *The New Reformation*, 115.

81. Greg Ogden does not mention the title New Apostolic Paradigm or New Apostolic Reformation. However, the title of his book is New Reformation.

82. Ogden, *The New Reformation*, 177; Trueblood, *La Iglesia: Un Compañerismo Incendiario*, 37–38.

dissension. Each denomination tries to do its part for the kingdom of God, but at the same time feeling sentiments of competition or rivalry.

Denominations are also subject to authority because of the rules. Authority is centralized on a figure. As Towns recalls history, authority was centralized on the bishop, and those bishops of large cities had more authority than others, as was the case of the bishop of Rome.[83] Denominations are also built on a committee or board of director's base, who also "elect" leaders and also have the authority to fire them.[84]

Networks in the NAP, as opposed to denominations, are built upon the base of relationships.[85] Cannistraci says that the difference between denominations and apostolic networks is relationships, rather than "policies and rules." Relationships become the source of strength accomplished by "partnership of prayer, discussion, planning, and visionary leadership."[86]

Apostolic networks are the result of unity. They are associations of "autonomous churches and individual ministries that are voluntarily united in an organized structure."[87] Authority is not positional, but relational. Network leaders have authority not because of their position, but because network members voluntarily submit themselves on the basis of trust. Because the sole purpose of the network is to serve local congregations, and not to exercise authority over them, they have a "philosophy of servanthood."[88]

Because relationships are the foundations of the network, the practice of relationships must be real, not merely attested on the statement of faith. Relationships are essential if the church is considered as a body whereas, in an organization, rules and control are the characteristic. The clear mission and purpose of the network is the expansion of the kingdom of God. This is accomplished by having as a central focus church planting and multiplication, world missions and outreach, as elements to fulfill the Great Commission. Therefore, the essential priorities of an apostolic network are that of relationships, equipping, multiplication, and mission.[89]

---

83. Towns, *Is the Day of the Denomination Dead?*, 61.
84. Wagner, *Churchquake*, 27–28, 82–84.
85. Ibid., 127–28.
86. Cannistraci, *Apostles and the Emerging Apostolic Movement*, 190.
87. Ibid.
88. Ibid., 190–91; Wagner, *Churchquake*, 127–32;
89. Cannistraci, *Apostles and the Emerging Apostolic Movement*, 192–94.

ESCHATOLOGY IN THE NEW APOSTOLIC PARADIGM

Bosch names four eschatological models that had an impact on missionary thinking in recent years: that of Karl Barth, Rudolph Bultmann, Paul Althans and Oscar Cullmann. The fourth model, Oscar Cullmann's, has a greater impact because it considers the kingdom of God as a hermeneutical key. The kingdom of God is present, and it is also future. Mission then is a preparation for the end. He also notes that the eschatological element is not only a motivation for mission, but in many cases it has paralyzed mission. However, Bosch finds a creative tension between eschatology and mission. This is a kind of eschatology that is future oriented but present at the same time; one that considers the kingdom as here and now but as not yet; one, he says, that sees the new age closer, but with the old one not ended yet. It is an eschatology based on hope; the hope of the Christian who knows that Christ is coming back again, and the victory of those who believe and who patiently work taking the mission of God.[90]

The eschatological element plays an important role in the NAP. The reason is a new hermeneutic. Traditionally, the interpretation of times has been by taking the past to understand the present. In the NAP the future is considered in order to understand the present, reading the signs of the times in the Bible to understand the future, and applying them to understand the present. This is now the missional drive in the NAP: the realization that we live in the end times and the return of the Lord is closer now. The kingdom of God is here, is seen in a Protestantism that submits to the lordship of Christ in an active way, but is not yet because the King has not physically come.[91]

The realization that the end of times is near is what moves people to reach others with the gospel. Just like the Apostolic Paradigm, Christians now in the NAP consider themselves as the last generation before Christ's coming. Eschatology in the NAP is not a realized eschatology. It is an expectant one, based on the blessed hope of the return of Christ to reign among his people.

Another eschatological event characteristic of the NAP is expectancy of a worldwide revival, a revival that will take place before the coming of the Lord. This is a revival like no other in history—a revival that begins

---

90. Bosch, *Transforming Mission*, 501, 503–4, 507–10; Wagner, *Churchquake*, 70–71.

91. Deiros, *Protestantismo en América Latina*, 127–28; "The Roots and Fruits of the Argentine Revival," 49–50.

with the renewal of the church in the power of the Spirit. This means the practice of the same traditional theology but with a different understanding under a new paradigm.

Reports of revivals became more common in the 1990s. College revivals were reported on different campuses. There were city-wide revivals such as the Toronto Airport Vineyard known as the "Toronto Blessing;" the "ecumenical revival with emphasis on evangelism and signs and wonder" of Melbourne, Florida; the revival at the Brownsville Assembly of God in Pensacola, Florida; the Men's revival with groups such as Promise Keepers; the Argentine revival with a renewal in spiritual warfare, prayer, and most of all, the restoration of the apostolic ministry. Such are the examples of the growing expectancy of a worldwide revival before the coming of the Lord in fulfillment of biblical prophecy. Such revivals awake the church's self-understanding of being the church and of its mission.[92]

MISSIOLOGY IN THE NEW APOSTOLIC PARADIGM

It is out of the ecclesiology in the NAP that missiology emerges. The shift in the concept of the church also brings a shift in the "missional reality" of the local congregation.[93]

Bosch notes that in order to understand the shifts in Missiological thinking, it is important to consider the significant world missionary congresses, and what is the relationship between the church and mission, Christian and non-Christian countries, the church and the world.

By 1952 at the Willingen congress of the International Missionary Council (ICM), the debate continued with the assumption that the emphasis of mission was centered in the church. It is at Willingen that a new approach to mission emerges, considering now the church neither as the center, nor as the objective of mission, but as one and the same in the *Missio Dei*. The mission of God is the mission of the church and the mission of the church is the mission of God. The church is the mission, and because the church is everywhere, missionary headquarters are everywhere.[94]

---

92. Damazio, *Seasons of Revival*, 37–54; Wagner, "Revival Power," 8–10; Deiros, *Protestantismo en América Latina*, 89–91; Cannistraci, *Apostles and the Emerging Apostolic Movement*. 19.

93. Mays, "After Christendom, What?," 245–55.

94. Bosch, *Transforming Mission*, 369–71; Mays, "After Christendom, What?," 250–51.

In the NAP the church is missionary in nature. There is no mission without the church and no church without mission. The church commissions and is commissioned. The missionary nature of the church is evidenced by how the church glorifies God in worship, community, and witness; where the ministry is decentralized among the members of the body and where the church intentionally involves itself in bringing the gospel to the community it serves.[95]

Mead notes that the missionary shift of the church in the NAP has several implications beyond the ministry of all believers. First, believers cannot assume that all are Christians because they live in the same community, as was the case in Christendom. Second, believers cannot assume that all in the community live according to biblical values and morals; and third, as in the case of the Apostolic Paradigm, the church now considers its doors as the gateway to the missionary field.[96]

Having Mead's view in mind, two major aspects can summarize the missiology of the NAP: the incarnational and the global. This means that mission cannot be divorced either from the local community, or from the global outreach. There is a similitude of today's world and that of the Apostolic Paradigm. Today's world is also "pagan and pluralistic" where the question is no longer whether God exists, but how God is different from other gods.[97] This brings about a new missionary zeal in the local congregation, which is not contented with sending offerings to the denominational mission's center, but wants to take an active role in reaching new cultures.[98]

In the NAP mission is not only a faraway enterprise—going where nobody has gone before. It begins with evangelizing the church and its own culture as well. True mission begins at the local level and extends to the world. Therefore, a new priority must occupy the first place, which is "context over structure." The agenda of the church is set by people's needs, not by the needs of the institution. The church in mission is in the outward looking mode.[99]

---

95. Ibid., 373; Snyder, *Radical Renewal*, 119–25.
96. Mead, *The Once and Future Church*, 25.
97. Rainer, *Giant Awakenings*, 148–49.
98. Wagner, *Churchquake*, 186.
99. Deiros, "The Roots and Fruits of the Argentine Revival," 51–52; Wagner, *Churchquake*, 69–70.

Missiology on the global aspect also takes the form of church planting. People in the church "avoid the 'bless me syndrome' as they try to live up to their apostolic nature and calling." This does not mean that Christians don't want to be blessed; it means that they want to be blessed only as a mean to reach others with the good news of Christ. Church planting is assumed as part of the mission of the church.[100]

The incarnational aspect of the church in mission takes the role of social service. As previously mentioned, the needs of the people set the agenda for the church in mission. These needs are not only spiritual, but also physical and material. The mission of the church is also understood as that of reaching the poor, the needy and the outcast of society. However, this is not seen as "social action" implying a sociopolitical involvement of the church, but that of the gift of mercy exercised by the local congregation.[101]

An important feature of missiology in the NAP is that of a balance between the cultural mandate and the evangelistic mandate. The predominance of either one has also been an important item of discussion in the different missionary congresses of the twentieth century. The point is that the mission of God is both, evangelistic in reaching people lost in sin, and cultural or social, in showing the love of God.

Evangelization and social responsibility are both part of the church in mission. Evangelization will produce social involvement seeking the welfare of people. A convergence of convictions came out of the Wheaton Conference in 1983, where the mission of the church was to be understood as both evangelization and the demonstration of the gospel.[102]

This is the case of the NAP. Churches in the NAP see sin as the cause of social problems. Seeing sin as the cause of social problems, the church understands that evangelization is the cure, not the implementation of more social programs. However, mission is understood as showing the love of God in different ways such as the implementation of "mercy

---

100. Wagner, "The New Apostolic Reformation," 24; Easum, *Dancing With Dinosaurs*, 108–9.

101. Wagner, *Churchquake*, 195–98. Van Engen considers the role of the local congregation as prophetic, priestly, and kingly, as well as that of healer and liberator following Christ's mission of Luke 4:18–19 (*God's Missionary People*, 119–30).

102. Bosch, *Transforming Mission*, 403–8.

ministries," not only as means to fulfill the social mandate, but also the evangelistic mandate.[103]

In reading church history, one can see the different developments resulting in paradigm shifts in the church's self-understanding of being the church and of mission. The history of the church in mission has always been a struggle to carry out a two sided commission, that of being a witness to the world, to convert and to save the world, and at the same time, to be different from the world.[104]

Throughout the centuries the history of the church has been one of changes: different developments, changes in direction, power struggles, times of change and confusion; but with always one focus—mission. It is about the recent changes in the church that I want to devote the next chapter. This chapter will provide a historical survey of recent events in the twentieth century, secular and religious, that led to the present state of the church as a result of a recent paradigm shift, as well as tracing the emergence of the New Apostolic Churches.

---

103. Wagner, *Churchquake*, 195–200.
104. Mead, *The Once and Future Church*, 9.

5

A Transforming Revolution

AS WAS THE CASE of the Protestant Reformation, several similar causes are taking place in today's society that call for a transformation and renewal of the church. Political, moral, and intellectual, changes in the social structure of the time, and the failure of the traditional church in meeting people's needs are some examples of the similarities with the Reformation of the sixteenth century.[1]

Like Miller points out, American Protestantism is experiencing a transforming revolution. Even though mainline churches are losing members, church attendance is not declining. People are attending a new style of congregation forming in the United States in response to the many changes experienced after the 1960s cultural shift.[2]

In this chapter I will deal with topics such as the effects of postmodernism, globalization, networking, and post-institutionalization, as well as other secular events in the 1980s and 1990s that affected the church.

GENERAL BACKGROUND

The 1980s set the background for the major paradigm shift that would affect the world as a whole. Many of the important changes would take place in the United States As one of the world's economic leaders, innovations taking place in the United States would also affect the world's

---

1. Cairnes, *Christianity Through the Centuries*, 278–81.
2. Miller, *Reinventing American Protestantism*, 1.

economy. The same is true for Europe, which changes would reach the United States also.

One of these major changes is postmodernism. Postmodernism, originally coined as a way to describe reactive tendencies to modernism by Federico de Onis in the 1930s, did not gain prominence until the cultural revolution of the 1960s, especially in the arts and literature, and later in the 1970s in architecture. However, it wasn't until the 1980s that postmodernism took a different meaning, that of a new worldview that embraces different aspects such as "philosophy, the arts, politics, and certain branches of science, theology and popular culture."[3]

The term postmodernism in the literary arts has been used as a "conservative reaction within modernism." It also marks a historical period and an aesthetic style, as a concept of different "and beyond the modern . . . a variant of the modern."[4]

Furthermore, postmodernism must be understood as "resistance and reaction." Barry Smart calls for a distinction between postmodernism as resistance and postmodernism as reaction. The first one resists the modern and the status quo, and the second one repudiates the modern and celebrates the status quo. In philosophy and social theory, postmodernism considers that the modern has reached the limits, because modernity has failed in achieving its promises of redeeming humankind from its afflictions of poverty and ignorance and prejudice, therefore something new must come into place.[5]

Effects of Postmodernism

In the middle of the twentieth century a change began to take place, from modernity to postmodernity. This process began to take place in the 1960s when young people began to look for relevancy and selfhood. However, this search gave way to a fissure in the culture, characterized mainly by personhood and autonomy spreading to the rest of society.[6] It is a major "cultural shift of seismic proportions" to the point of paralyzing, by the

---

3. Gibbs, *ChurchNext*, 23.
4. Smart, "Modernity, Postmodernity and the Present," 21.
5. Ibid., 24–25.
6. The Third Reformed Church—Holland, "The Post-modern Culture," n.p.

"shock waves" it sends, anyone who is not aware of it. It is a change in worldview because it is a change in the deep roots of culture.[7]

Postmodernism is characterized mainly by a rejection of the institutional, materialistic and scientific reasoning. This movement sees a lack of emotions and spiritual fulfillment.[8] In postmodernism there is no truth, but there are truths because "true Truth has never been ours."[9]

An important characteristic of postmodernism is the new hermeneutics of reality. That is the way to understand reality, and where language plays an important role in the way of constructing reality, which is created by those who have the power—those who control the official language.

The power-knowledge is also important to understand and interpret the text; it is a linguistic move into philosophy. However, the way to neutralize reality is by deconstruction. In some way, deconstruction is being fair to others in our speech, or being politically correct in our language.[10]

Postmodernism affects every aspect of culture. Therefore, its effects are felt in the same way sooner or later. For example, postmodernism is often associated with a consumer society, because of the life-style and the consumption in mass that dominates "taste and fashion."[11]

Postmodern society has become pessimistic and skeptic. In this era, people tend to question ideas and statements. There is a continual rejection of propositional truths and a need to look for reasons behind what is proposed. There is a tendency to question and examine things and not take them for granted.[12]

Because postmodernism has abandoned truth in search for reasons for the truth, postmodern culture is a pragmatic one. Pragmatism is a very clear effect of postmodernism, and the idea is "whatever works for you."[13] The practical side is more valuable than bureaucratic procedures.

---

7. Gibbs, *ChurchNext*, 19.

8. The Third Reformed Church—Holland, "The Post-modern Culture," n.p.

9. Hurd, "Postmodernism," McKenzie Study Center Online (1998). Google. Accessed 5/3/2001.

10. Grassie, "Postmodernism: What One Needs to Know," in *Zygon: Journal of Religion and Science* Online: http://mckenziestudycenter.org/2001/02/postmodernism/; Hurd, "Postmodernism: A New Model of Reality," n.p.

11. Turner, "Periodization and Politics in the Postmodern," 3.

12. Gibbs, *ChurchNext*, 23, 212.

13. Ibid., 24.

This in turns leads to a decentralize system of organization as a way of reacting against traditional organization and institutionalization.[14]

Individualism is an effect of postmodernism also. However, individualism does not mean isolation of the person, but that each one is entitled to look for "his or her own meaning" in life and to relate with others as one desires. Individualism also means that each person is entitled to his or her own opinion, and to share it with others in the fragmented society one lives. Postmodern people do not live in isolation; they take advantage of the Internet. It is the way postmodernists mingle with others and share their individual opinions.[15]

Because of the Internet, postmodernism has its effects also in the virtual culture developed after the World Wide Web (WWW). People in postmodern society tend to live a virtual reality, because reality is given to society via the informational media, cyberspace or TV. This Age of informational speed also creates a virtual reality life. That is, people by perceiving the images transmitted via TV or the Internet, immediately live them out, as if they were present at the time and place of the happening.[16]

Eddie Gibbs, in *ChurchNext*, presents some of the effects of postmodernism. Some of these are: suspicion of institutions due to the loss of confidence; decentralized networks, the unpredictability of life that makes planning difficult leading to a "plan-do" attitude; and insecurity of the present and fear of what the future might hold along with "pessimism and paranoia."[17]

Furthermore, postmodernist culture is in the quest for a transcendental experience. Experience has a higher value than knowledge. In the church, for example, the effects of postmodernism are felt in the worship styles of today's generation, seeking a spiritual experience, rather than rational worship.[18] This has given way, in a postmodernist society, to the rise of many spiritual movements, self-help groups, personal growth and development groups, yoga groups, and other similar ones.[19]

---

14. Miller, *Reinventing American Protestantism*, 136, 140–42.
15. Gibbs, *ChurchNext*, 24.
16. Hong, *Una Iglesia Posmoderna*, 20–21.
17. Gibbs, *ChurchNext*, 25.
18. Ibid., 160–62; Miller, *Reinventing American Protestantism*, 145–46.
19. The Third Reformed Church—Holland, "The Post-modern Culture."

The person is seen as a whole, made up of body, soul and will. There is an attempt to bring together the rational with emotional, spirit mind and intellect, technology and personhood.[20]

In his book *Una Iglesia Posmoderna? (A Postmodern Church?)*, Sik Hong analyzes postmodernism and the postmodern person. Hong considers that postmodern spirituality has different facets, such as being subjective. Each person is in search of a personal religious experience, and not a hereditary one. It is also emotional, meaning a tendency to search for community and sense of belonging, however, with a tendency to reject the "doctrinal and dogmatic"; Spirituality can be tribal and, in this sense, it becomes "nationalistic" in some way and can be expressed as "sect-like." It is ecumenical and syncretistic of indifference, wherein postmodern spirituality sees all religions guiding people to the same end, and there is no monopolization of religion. Therefore, "a postmodern person can be a Christian and at the same time believe in reincarnation."[21]

Globalization

Even though it is difficult to trace the actual beginnings of globalization, the historical trends after WWII and the end of the Cold War are, to a certain point, the roots for the creation of a global civilization. However, there is no actual date that marks the beginning of globalization as such. Some believe that globalization began as a wider outreach of the United States after the collapse of the Soviet Union, and through the support, by the United States of its allies as instruments of "global hegemony."[22]

The economists' view of globalization goes back to the 1970s. However, in recent developments of the 1980s and 1990s, globalization took an economic meaning,[23] giving in this way a different understanding of the matter, and leading only the ones interested in economy to pursue a deeper understanding of such an important development of the late twentieth century.

Globalization is a multidimensional process that involves the cultural, economic, and political at the same time. It is a "compression of the

---

20. Gibbs, ChurchNext, 170; The Third Reformed Church—Holland, "The Postmodern Culture."
21. Hong, *Una Iglesia Posmoderna?*, 10–15.
22. Stackhouse, "General Introduction," 8n9.
23. Robertson, "Globalization and the Future of Traditional Religion," 54–55.

world," and it is different from global integration. It is an interrelated process that has culminated in the breaking of barriers involving "industrial, economic, technological, cultural, and cognitive," and which becomes permeable to distances.[24]

John Naisbitt, in *Megatrends*, calls for a change in attitude, realizing that yesterday is over. Therefore, we must make the necessary adjustments for a different kind of economy, one of "a world of interrelated communities."[25]

The advances in communication technology have made globalization possible. Today it is possible to know what is happening around the world in a few minutes, just by switching channels on TV or by surfing the Internet. Regional boundaries have been broken because of the advances of communications, and today, villages, peoples of different cultures, and entire nations that were once contained to their own world, are now aware of each other's existence. In economic terms, the advances of communications have made today's economy a world economy, namely because satellite communications have collapsed the "communication float"—the time between which information is sent and received has shortened.[26]

Globalization as an economic trend has to do with alliances made by manufacturers with other businesses. In economic terms, globalization means mutual cooperation including other nations in the manufacture of goods. The global car is a clear example. This is a car built with parts made in different countries, and shipped to a central location where it is finally assembled.[27]

Naisbitt presents some of the characteristics of globalization, such as global interdependence. This means that industrial countries establish relationships with Third World countries because of the need of each other. Developed countries, such as the United States, do not see Third World countries on a moral basis as poor neighbors, but as interdependent. Globalization, says Naisbitt, is accompanied by a cultural renaissance. Cultures are reaffirmed. There is a strong emphasis on nationalism. However, a cultural renaissance also means the use of a common language. In this case, English has become a global language, making globalization

---

24. Ibid., Arthur, *The Globalization of Communications*, 3.
25. Naisbitt, *Megatrends*, 53.
26. Arthur, *The Globalization of Communications*, 4; Naisbitt, *Megatrends*, 57.
27. Naisbitt, *Megatrends*, 71–72.

easier. "Cultures of English-speaking countries will dominate."[28] It is considered as a truly universal language, spoken even more than Mandarin Chinese, and learned in schools as required language in several countries, such as Hong Kong, France, and Japan. Nevertheless, a cultural renaissance also implies the use of computer language, which in this technological day and age has also become a must. Globalization also calls for peace—global peace. It is a way of uniting people to solve conflicts and to think on a large scale for a larger benefit.[29]

Also important to note is that globalization has its effects in the use of a global language. As previously mentioned, English has become a global language. In the information age, English is used as a common language, to the point that computers talk between them in English, and computer programs are in English. English is the business language of today's world economy. It is the language of preference for international businesses to write memorandums and to strike deals. It is also the language of diplomacy, and the one used among people in countries where they speak different languages.

However, globalization is not only the exportation or the use of a common language, but also of a common culture. The internationalization of young culture from the United States is also an important trend of globalization. Music, dance, performers, and athletes, as well as new sports such as surfing and bodybuilding, are also examples of how globalization affects the world as a whole.[30]

Naisbitt and Aburdene consider individualization as a byproduct of globalization. Individualization is a reaction of triumph against the "anonymity of the collective." As a counterpart of the collective, individuals have the potential to become more responsible, as oppose of hiding oneself among the whole. However, individualization does not mean isolation, but it is a way to search for community, which is different from the collective. Community is "the free association of individuals." Thus individuals who want to excel seek community; those who want to hide from responsibility seek the refuge in the collective.[31]

---

28. Naisbitt and Aburdene, *Megatrends 2000*, 139.
29. Naisbitt, *Megatrends*, 76–79; Naisbitt and Aburdene, *Megatrends 2000*, 139–40.
30. Naisbitt and Aburdene, *Megatrends 2000*, 141–42.
31. Ibid., 299–300.

Networking

The 1960s and 1970s saw the smashing of the pyramid style of organization; even though hierarchies still exist people do not believe in their efficacy anymore. This led to talking to one another in order to solve society's problems; and a new and still emerging trend in our day, affecting businesses, politics, and communications gave way to networking.[32]

Networks are powerful tools for social action. For example, the women's movement emerged as a classic network, by women and for women talking to each other and sharing information, altering in this way the way women are seen traditionally. Likewise, the anti-war and environmental movements of the 1960s and 1970s started when people began to share common interests and concerns.[33]

Networks are the first steps in a community's start of a self-help group, as opposed to institutional help. Networks are a reaction to the lack of needs fulfilled by the traditional institutions. It is a revolutionary trend that is rapidly replacing the traditional hierarchical organizational system. One of the main reasons is productivity. Networks principles are productive tools to achieve common goals.[34]

According to Naisbitt, networks are chains of people talking to each other, through informal communication in a horizontal way, sharing information, ideas, and resources towards a common goal.[35] This method has proven to be successful in different businesses and large corporations such as Honeywell, Intel, and Hewlett Packard.[36]

Important in a network is not the network itself, but the process that takes place in connecting people. In the classical sense of the definition, networks "never grow into the organization stage." That is, networks never become organizations; otherwise they cease to be networks. The whole purpose of a network is the sharing of information, fostering self-help, and solving society's problems improving productivity, quality work life, and the sharing of resources.[37]

---

32. Naisbitt, *Megatrends*, 212; Cannistraci, *Apostles and the Emerging Apostolic Movement*, 186.

33. Ibid., 214; Pousson, *Spreading the Flame*, 63.

34. Naisbitt, *Megatrends*, 215; Cannistraci, *Apostles and the Emerging Apostolic Movement*, 187.

35. Naibitt, *Megatrends*, 215.

36. Pousson, *Spreading the Flame*, 62.

37. Naibitt, *Megatrends*, 216.

Networks are also a reaction against institutionalism, because institutions have failed to fulfill people's needs. For this reason, networking is also an effect of postmodernism in today's society. Networks are also a multitude of cells (groups) of different sizes linked together to each other in a direct or indirect way.

Networks emerge when people try to change society where traditional institutions have failed. Then people under a common goal or cause get together to share ideas and resources to fulfill that goal. They also get together under the same beliefs, no matter if those believes are social, political, or religious.

Networks involve people on every level, giving networks another characteristic: networks that are egalitarian instead of elitist. Naisbitt also gives three fundamental reasons for networking emerging "as a critical social form now: (1) the death of traditional institutions, (2) the din of information overload, and (3) the past failure of hierarchies."[38]

Also important to note is that networks emerge within traditional institutions. As previously mentioned, it is the failure of traditional institutions in fulfilling people's needs that gives way to people within the organization to look for help or information, or whatever is needed for them to succeed in society, outside the traditional institution. This is the first step towards the birth of a network.

An important aspect of networking is also the fact that American society has become a mobile society, meaning that people tend to move geographically more often than they used to, because of the advances in urbanization. People's need for a sense of belonging can be met in a network.[39]

Post-Institutionalization

The prefix *post* at first look in the word *post-institutionalization* calls the attention of the reader to conclude that it means "against institutionalization." However, it should be understood that the literal meaning of the prefix is "after, later or posterior to" deriving from the Latin *post* that means 'after.'[40]

As is the case of postmodernism, many consider this trend as against modernism, but there are others that consider it as after modernism.

---

38. Ibid., 219–20.
39. Ibid., 221–28.
40. "Post," in *Encarta Encyclopedia*, n.p.

However the case, the prefix 'post' has the intended meaning of 'after', or it may also be interpreted as a reaction to. It looks back to where it is coming from, and at the same time it looks forward to what is after. Therefore, the prefix *post* should not be interpreted as the prefix *anti*.[41]

Institution on the other hand, is something already established. In this case, post-institutionalization is a reaction to what is already established. As a reaction, post-institutionalization should not be understood as against institutions, but as what comes after institutions. That is, the next step after the traditional view of institutions.

As Naisbitt describes the developing trend of going from institutional help to self-help, it was during the 1970s that Americans started to disengage from institutions. For decades, Americans had trusted the institutional system, depending on it for many of their needs. It was during the Great Depression of the 1930s that Americans began to lose faith in them, and as a traumatic event, Americans sought the most needed strength in the large institutions. However, at various points in time, people began to experience the failure of traditional institutions in fulfilling their needs. The Vietnam War was a turning point and a discouraging element at the same time. Along with this, in the 1970s, was also the failure of the educational system with lower SAT scores, beginning a trend of decline. Nonetheless, this trend was not a lost cause, because this trend brought a self-sufficient / self-interest motivation that led people to seek each other for help, sharing ideas and resources to fulfill their needs. People within traditional institutions began to look for help outside the boundaries, giving way to what is known as networking.[42]

As noted above, Post-institutionalization does not mean against institutions, but it is a reaction to the failure of the traditional institutional system. Nonetheless, we can say that post-institutionalization is truly a reaction against institutionalism. When organizations of any sort settle in a certain stage of their life and begin to work in developing better or different policies that build up the organization, instead of developing better or different ways to reach people in their needs, they become institutionalized. It is against this that people react.

---

41. Bosch, *Misión en Transformación*, 427n1.
42. Naisbitt, *Megatrends*, 143–74.

Other Secular Events in the 1980s and 1990s[43]

The 1980s and 1990s were two decades of important developments in the transition into a new paradigm. They were the decades of major paradigm shifts because of the coming of the new millennium. Trends that began to develop in the mid-twentieth century began to emerge with more clarity in these two decades. These trends would set the stage for life in the new millennium.

John Naisbitt and Patricia Aburdene in their book *Megatrends 2000*, a sequel to the original *Megatrends* (1984), in which Naisbitt forecast major changes that would take place in the 1980s, changes in preparation for the new millennium. The book describes the most important trends of the 1990s. According to Naisbitt and Aburdene, the 1990s would be a decade of important technological changes without precedence and of major developments from politics to the arts.[44]

One of the major changes in American society was that of going from being an industrial society to that of an information society. The industrial era of the early twentieth century began to shift by the late 1950s, when information began to be a key factor in American society. The launching of satellites played a major role in the information society, which is characterized by "innovations in communications and computer technology," collapsing the information float; that is, the time between the messages sent and received. Therefore, speed of communications is essential in an information society.[45]

The 1980s were also the decade of "the home computer explosion,"[46] a major factor in the paradigm shift of the decade. Computers that were virtually unavailable to people, not only because of the expertise needed to use them, but also because of price and space, became available to consumers due to reduction of price, as well as the availability of user-friendly software developed. Computers in an information society are as important as cars were in the industrial society of the past. Computers became the vehicle of travel in the information society, shortening not only

---

43. Even though there were other important trends and events in American society during the 1980s and 1990s, I'm only dealing with those that have a more direct relationship to the present research, and which had a more direct influence on the emergence of NACs.

44. As Deiros describes it in, *Protestantismo en América Latina*, 82.

45. Naisbitt, *Megatrends*, 14–18.

46. Ibid., 18.

the time of communications, but also the space traveled. In an industrial society, people dealt with physical space traveled by car, whereas in an information society, people deal with conceptual space (virtual space), traveled by computer communications via modems.[47]

Another of the major trends of the 1980s and 1990s is that of decentralization. Decentralization is a move away from a centralized type of organization, where a person or a group of persons do most of the work. Decentralization is the way people react to institutionalism, and it affects every aspect of society, from politics to business to every aspect of culture. In a decentralized society people move away from the urban to the suburban, to small towns. There is also a tendency to stress the differences rather than the similarities. In other words, a decentralized society is a diversified society.[48]

Decentralization is also a way for people to react to the lack of an "effective top-down solution." This resulted in people taking action in political activities, organizing themselves for local action. This in turn resulted in the organization of people in their neighborhoods taking action on the local levels to tackling the most important problems such as education, crimes, and waste disposal.[49]

Socialism in the 1990s also saw the importance of decentralization, when "free-market socialism" began to emerge as a way to salvage socialism. Several are the factors for the demise of socialism, among them, "the failure of centralization." Under Mikhail Gorbachev, the Soviets conceded to the idea of a "decentralized, entrepreneurial, market-driven model" as more effective than the command economy they had had since the days of Stalin. Along the lines is also the high cost of a centralized government supplied social services, which in the minds of many government leaders is overwhelming and leading to bankruptcy.[50]

Centralization is also an unfavorable factor for democracy. "Strong central leadership is anathema to democracy," says Naisbitt. This in turns leads to the development of a more participatory democracy instead of a representative one. In a participatory democracy, people have a saying

---

47. Ibid., 18–33.
48. Ibid., 103–4.
49. Ibid., 120–26.
50. Naisbitt and Aburdene, *Megatrends 2000*, 93–94.

in what is being done, in "business, government or the marketplace."[51] The basic principle is that people have a part in deciding how to arrive to a certain decision that affects their life. In a representative democracy, people elect others to make those decisions. In a representative democracy, leaders tell people how to do their jobs. However in a participatory democracy, leaders take into consideration people's input in how to perform their jobs uniting efforts for the common vision in order to attain a common goal. In this kind of environment, leaders develop people's skills in decision making, giving the leader the opportunity to become a more effective leader, facilitating things, instead of giving orders.[52]

The 1990s have also seen the emergence of a global lifestyle, thanks to globalization, and as an effect of globalization. Trademarks and corporations are imposing a global lifestyle because of the speed in travel and information. People in Japan are aware of what is happening in the American culture through film and television, to the point that "nearly 3 million Japanese visited the United States in 1988," many of them as "honeymooners."[53]

Teenage fashion is also part of the global lifestyle, favoring especially international fashion traders such as "Benetton, Espirit, or Laura Ashley."[54] This has also given way to global pricing. In today's world, prices are regulated electronically in order to deal with local currency variations that could drastically affect businesses.[55]

To this point I have dealt with the secular events and trends that make a general background, setting the stage for a major paradigm shift that would eventually reach the religious aspect of the American culture. However, one of the major trends predicted by Naisbitt and Aburdene is that of a religious revival without precedence in the 1990s. These events and trends set the stage for the emergence of the New Apostolic Churches, which I will deal with in the next section, dealing specifically with the religious background of the 1990s.

---

51. Naisbitt, *Megatrends*, 175.

52. Ibid., 175–209.

53. Naisbitt and Aburdene, *Megatrends 2000*, 121.

54. Ibid., 129.

55. Ibid., 118, 121, 129–33.

RELIGIOUS BACKGROUND

The secular events and general trends in the 1980s and 1990s help to set the stage for what was also happening in the religious arena during the same decades. The last decade of the second millennium, the 1990s, would serve as platform for the launching of a new religious paradigm, that could eventually change the way people and local congregations relate to each other and to the way Christianity is practiced and experienced.

Global Revival

The 1990s showed signs of a global religious revival without precedence, a kind of revival of a "worldwide multidenominational" scale. During this time, the baby boomer generation that rejected traditional organized religion in the 1970s would come back to religion, bringing their children either to church or to join a New Age group.[56] Even though Naisbitt and Aburdene are not Christian in the evangelical sense, they have seen a spiritual trend that leads towards a spiritual awakening of global proportions. There is an increment of the spiritual and the mystic as well as an increment of young people seeking a personal spiritual experience.[57]

Because the 1990s were the last decade of the millennium, religious belief intensified around the world. This is a common trend at the end of a millennium when people begin to think of the end times. The millennium is compared to the thousand years of reign of Christ on earth with His people, which marks the golden era in human history. However, this also brought the idea of the end of the world, such as it was at the end of the 990s, when in the Dark Ages people approaching the end of the first millennium thought "the end of the world was at hand" and early Christians though the end of the "millennium would rescue them of the Roman persecution." The same thing happened at the end of the 1990s; people believed it was the end of times, and the end of a millennium is a time of changes that brings hopes for some and desperation for others. Whatever is the case this time of changes brings up in people the need for a religious experience.[58]

One of the characteristics of the 1990s was the decline of mainline denominations. However, this does not mean that people are not interested

---

56. Ibid., 270.
57. Deiros, *Protestantismo en América Latina*, 87.
58. Naisbitt and Aburdene, *Megatrends 2000*, 270–72.

in the spiritual, but it is a rejection of organized religion. Americans are not considered as religious people, but as spiritual ones, not belonging to a church or a particular religion. People seek peace and well being and that is why they turn to religion; however they are not finding it in religious organizations, which are more concerned with the organizational aspect of their group, rather than with the theological or the spiritual.

This in turn has giving way to the development of new groups outside mainline religions, such as Roman Catholics, Protestant and Jewish groups. New groups have sprouted more in the fashion of "made-in-America" style; different groups that go from Black Muslims, to Buddhist chaplains being recognized by the armed forces in the United States, to Korean churches from the Korean World Mission Council.[59]

Naisbitt and Aburdene also mention the growth of the New Age movement. A movement that is difficult to measure because there are no membership lists, but a movement that "represent 5 to 10 percent of the population." Even though the New Age movement is not an organized religion, the Unity Church is the closest thing to it.

The 1990s was also the decade of catching up for mainline denominations. The religious revival brought an awakening of the spiritual among the mainline denominations. Catholics as well as Protestants began to reflect more openly their charismatic experiences, going back to a personal conversion experience, the formation of home Bible study groups, development of alternative worship services, as well as joining the technological era through the use of the media.

Evangelical churches also developed different methodologies to reach out to the community. Using marketing strategies, evangelical churches around the United States have experienced significant growth, as in the case of Willow Creek Community Church in Illinois. There are some economic implications as well. Growing churches tend to build multi-million dollar structures to accommodate people, such as Orlando First Baptist Church who built a $14 million dollar structure; or the $20 million spent on Calvary Assembly's five thousand seat building in Orlando—which went from a membership of two thousand to six thousand in five years.[60]

The religious revival of the last two decades of the millennium also awaken, as previously mentioned, a thirst for the spiritual that reached

---

59. Ibid., 273–77.
60. Ibid., 280–97.

mainline as well as non-historic denominations. This spiritual awakening brought different charismatic manifestations that developed into different ways of expressions among Christians.

Charismatic Developments[61]

The 1980s and 1990s saw a charismatic development among different wings of Christianity. These charismatic developments did not start during these decades, but they trace their roots to the Charismatic movement of the 1960s, however, carrying a different worldview during this time and reaching different generations. There are three charismatic developments during these decades, which are: The Independent Charismatic, the Third Wave, and the Neo-Charismatics.

The Independent Charismatic

The Independent Charismatic movement traces its roots to the Second Wave or the Charismatic movement that gained prominence during the 1960s. The Second Wave is also a development of the Pentecostal movement (First Wave) of the early 1900s as a result of the Topeka, Kansas revival in 1901, and the 1906 Azusa Street revival.[62]

During the 1940s divine healing evangelists, such as Oral Roberts, T. L. Osborne and Gordon Lindsay spread the message of the baptism of the Spirit among Christians of different denominations. Believers of different backgrounds began to accept the Pentecostal experience, without being completely Pentecostal in doctrine. They accepted the speaking in tongues as evidence of being baptized with the Spirit, but not being the only evidence.

In 1959, an Episcopalian couple, John and Joan Baker, from a parish in Monterey Park, California, received the Baptism of the Holy Spirit. At first, they thought of leaving the Episcopal Church and joining a

---

61. I am using the term "charismatic" not so much in the historical sense of the word, but more in the etymological sense. Charismatic in this section refers to the different developments that took place during the 1980s and 1990s in relationship to an understanding and opening to the work of the Holy Spirit. A different understanding and practice of the gifts of the Spirit evidence the work of the Holy Spirit, which are experienced not only by the traditionally known Pentecostals, or Charismatics, but also by other Christians that do not identify with Pentecostal nor Charismatic. They are the Third Wave and the Neo-Charismatics or Christians of the New Paradigm, that in light of this study are part of the NACs.

62. Burgess, et al., "Introduction," 2–3.

Pentecostal congregation. However, they decided to stay and told their vicar, Frank Maguire, of their experience. Maguire sought the help of another pastor, Dennis Bennett, from St. Mark's Church in Van Nuys, California, and by the end of the year, both Maguire and Bennett had received the baptism of the Holy Spirit. During the Sunday morning service of April 3, 1960, Dennis Bennett announced to his congregation of this experienced, and of his resignation as vicar of St. Mark's Church, but not of the Episcopal Church.[63]

By 1990, the Charismatic movement (Second Wave), including both the main denominations as well as the independent or nondenominational charismatics, reached a total of over 140 million members. The Charismatic movement was considered as a reformist movement among historic denominations, because people who had received a charismatic experience did not want to leave their denominations, but to reform or renew the institutions "by the charismatic activity of the Holy Spirit."

However, the increasing opposition from their peers eventually forced them to leave their denominations, but at the same time, they did not want to affiliate with classical Pentecostals. One of these examples is the case of John Osteen who after receiving the baptism of the Holy Spirit, was forced to leave the Southern Baptists and found Lakewood Church, in Houston, Texas. Other Southern Baptists also followed Osteen's way in light of the schism. Similar things were happening among other denominations that opposed the renewal movement, and many new congregations were born, becoming known as Independent Charismatic.[64]

The Third Wave

The Third Wave is one of the most recent charismatic developments of the last decades of the twentieth century. The 1980s experienced another outpouring of the Holy Spirit among traditional denominations, and in 1983, Wagner coined the name "Third Wave" while he was being interviewed for *Pastoral Renewal* Magazine. Because it is a third wave, it also implies previous waves, and the term was coined with the specific purpose of distinguishing it from the previous ones. However, the Third Wave is a successor of the other two: of the First Wave, the Pentecostal movement;

63. Moriarty, *The New Charismatics*, 65, 69; Quebedeaux, *The New Charismatics II*, 61; Hocken, "Charismatic Movement," 130.

64. Quebedeaux, *The New Charismatics II*, 10; Pousson, *Spreading the Flame*, 34, 37–39.

and the Second Wave, the Charismatic movement. In spite of being different, the Third Wave also recognizes the work of the Holy Spirit as the other two movements did, but with some differences.[65]

This Third Wave of the Holy Spirit mainly involves Christians of traditional denominations who, having experienced the person of the Holy Spirit in a non-traditional way, don't want to identify themselves neither as Pentecostal nor Charismatic. The Third Wave is similar to and different from previous waves. It is similar because it is the same God at work, but different because of the understanding of the work of God through the Holy Spirit. The Third Wave doesn't see the ministry of the Holy Spirit as the end result, but within the ministry of the Spirit in the life of the believer is the healing of the sick, the casting out of demons, and other New Testament manifestations of signs and wonders. However, the main difference is in the "meaning of baptism in the Holy Spirit and the role of tongues in authenticating this"[66] baptism.[67]

Wagner in his book *The Third Wave of the Holy Spirit* (1988) gives a personal account of how he, being a traditional evangelical Christian, became empowered by the Holy Spirit in a totally different way as he had before. In this same book, Wagner tells his readers how he experienced the Holy Spirit, but didn't want to be labeled as Charismatic or Pentecostal, however, he says is open to the Holy Spirit's work. He also presents some of the main characteristics of the Third Wave, such as:

- Fourth Dimension Faith as one of the main characteristics of the Third Wave. It is called the shield of faith to resist (withstand) the attacks of the devil. It is used for spiritual warfare.

- The emphasis on signs and wonders, as well as the understanding of the continuous spiritual warfare.

- The miraculous power of the Holy Spirit "flowing in non-Pentecostal and non-Charismatic Churches."

- Engaging in Spiritual Warfare. This is not only the understanding of the reality of demons, but also defeating them with prayer and spiritual authority delegated to us.[68]

---

65. Moriarty, *The New Charismatics*, 101; Wagner, *The Third Wave of the Holy Spirit*, 13, 15.

66. Wagner, *The Third Wave of the Holy Spirit*, 18.

67. Deiros and Mraida, *Latinoamérica en Llamas*, 136.

68. Wagner, *The Third Wave of the Holy Spirit*, 22–24, 37–46, 51, 57–73.

The Third Wave emerges as a reaction to the formalism of the historic denominations that were not able to fulfill people's needs. People were tired of the formalism in worship and prayer presented in their congregations, as well as the nominal Christianity they lived. In light of this, and because people wanted a more charismatic type of worship service, many people decided to change their denominational affiliation, and as a reaction to this the Third Wave emerges and gains prominence.

The Third Wave is not a new denominational development of the 1980s, nor a new doctrinal development, but it is the practical application of what the Bible teaches about the Holy Spirit, his gifts, and of worship. Denominational churches related to the Third Wave remain in their denomination, but reflect in their worship services and their overall programs a more incarnational mission in and to the world.[69]

The Neo-Charismatics

Although the term "charismatic" in the historical sense is not new, it has become a describing word of the work of the Holy Spirit within the church. That is, where the teaching about the Holy Spirit takes precedence, where gifts of the Spirit are not only experienced, but the believers are also expected to practice them, and where the church is empowered and renewed for mission.

Important to note is the development from the First Wave (the Pentecostal movement) of several other charismatic movements. As previously mentioned, the Second Wave and the Third Wave are developments of classical Pentecostalism. Every charismatic movement that develops takes or is given a name to differentiate it from others. In some cases, the ones involved in the movement take a different name such is the case of the Third Wave, in which people don't want to be labeled as Pentecostal or as Charismatic.

Richard Quebedeaux gives an account of the development of the Charismatic movement in his book *The New Charismatics II*. In it, he shows how this movement of the Spirit became "part of the American religious mainstream." Quebedeaux uses the term Neopentecostal and charismatic interchangeably to name the movement that developed during the 1960s and to differentiate it from classical Pentecostalism. "New Chartismatics" for Quebedeaux is a term to name Christians who believe

---

69. Deiros and Mraida, *Latinoamérica en Llamas*, 138–39.

and practice the gifts of the Spirit, but it does not have any new connotation, other than a different movement from Pentecostalism.

Hong, in his book *Una Iglesia Posmoderna?* (A Postmodern Church?), on the other hand uses the term "neocharismatic" as synonymous with the Third Wave. For Hong the term describes believers of the Third Wave charismatic movement, and uses both terms interchangeably. Hong has borrowed the term from Quebedeaux and Moriarty.

Michael Moriarty uses the term "New Charismatics" with a different meaning than the previous ones. According to Moriarty, the New Charismatic movement is a development of the Second Wave (Charismatic movement). He gives this name to the movement[70] in light of the answer he got from the ones referred to as Charismatics, who "will plainly tell you that the charismatic movement is 'over.'"[71]

According to the proponents of the movement, God is starting a new move of the Holy Spirit within the church. God is triggering new and fresh ideas, bringing new teachings and new practices. One of the most prominent features of the Neo-Charismatics is the fast and progressive change of the teachings. The Neo-Charismatics are different in the teachings, in the new direction they are taking, as well as in their new agenda. It is the new agenda that also make the New-Charismatics somewhat controversial, due to the emphasis on restorationism; and because of this, they are considered as an expansion of the restoration or Latter Rain restorationism movement.[72]

Important features of the Neo-Charimatics are the emphasis on the restoration of the church. The church must be restored in full in all of its aspects, in order to be the mature and invincible church to fight against demonic powers. For this reason restoration of the fivefold ministry of Ephesians 4:11 is essential. Modern day apostles and prophets must be recognized as well. The full restoration of the church also includes the baptism of the Holy Spirit accompanied by supernatural manifestations, as well as a renewal of worship in the local church.[73]

---

70. Although the New Charismatics are new, even in the term describing them, it is a movement in the way that is "a multitude of people moving in the same general direction, and influencing one another." (O'Conner, *The Pentecostal Movement in the Catholic Church*, 33–34).

71. Moriarty, *The New Charismatics*, xii.

72. Ibid., xii, 84; Hong, *Una Iglesia Posmoderna?*, 33.

73. The baptism of the Holy Spirit is a common feature among classical Pentecostals,

Other features of the Neo-Charismatics are the unity of the church or unity of the faith. Unity of the church or of faith takes precedence among the Neo-Charismatics, rather than unity of doctrine. Unity is not equal to uniformity. Unity calls for the attainment of a common goal, while uniformity is everybody doing the same thing. Signs and wonders are also important features of the Neo-Charismatic movement, because there is a strong conviction that all of the signs, wonders, and spiritual gifts of the New Testament are still valid.[74]

Moriarty considers that the main feature of the Neo-Charismatics is the dominion pursuit. Kingdom theology is very prominent and Neo-Charismatics do not talk about the Rapture of the church as the classical Pentecostals did, but about restoration of the church, and that when everything is fully restored, the Lord will come back.[75] Some of the different charismatic movements that fall within the description of Neo-charismatics, according to Moriarty, are, "kingdom theology, the word of faith / positive confession movement, the Third Wave or signs and wonders movement, and the present-truth movement promoted by leaders such as Dick Iverson and Bill Hamon."[76]

Postdenominationalism

The Neo-Charismatics, as one of the latest developments of Christianity in the 1990s, in combination with the Independent Charismatics and the Third Wave opens a pathway in the mid-1990s to what became known as postdenominationalism. Although postdenominationalism as a name for a movement never became anything more than controversial, one cannot deny the fact that by the mid-1990s the denominational crisis was reaching a climax.[77]

Early in the 1970s, Towns perceived a trend among churches associated to a denomination as well as those considered as independent.

Charismatics, and the Neo-Charismatics. However, the difference lies in how the phrase is presented. Among Neo-Charismatics the phrase "baptism of or with the Holy Spirit" is replaced by "a visit of the Spirit" or "a move of the Spirit" or "filling of the Spirit." Also common is the term "the anointing" (Hong, *Una Iglesia Posmoderna?*, 33n13; Deiros and Mraida, *Latinoamérica en Llamas*, 146).

74. Hong, *Una Iglesia Posmoderna?*, 33–36; Moriarty, *The New Charismatics*, 85–112.
75. Moriarty, *The New Charismatics*, 87–88.
76. Ibid., xiii.
77. Wagner, *Churchquake*, 28–29.

Towns saw that those independent churches were growing and were vibrant because they carried out the Great Commission, and that mainline denominations were not expanding, rather, they were struggling to survive. Like Towns himself declares, he is not against denominations. He is against denominationalism, that is, the abuses of denominations.[78]

Leading Factors of Denominational Decline

The decline of denominations is nothing that should take anyone by surprise. When one considers the last half of the twentieth century, one can see that there were some factors that led to the denominational crisis.

Denominations were born out of conflict.[79] Theological struggles, doctrinal distinctives, and the confrontation of leaders led to separation. Some denominations were born because of differences in doctrines, while others were born because of doctrinal similarities. Some characterize themselves for being Calvinistic while others are Armenian. Liberalism is another factor. Liberalism within the church ranks leads to self-destruction. Along with liberalism there is a great skepticism among the clergy with respect to the great secular scandals of the "God is Dead" movement that reached the ranks of the clergy, developing skepticism with regards to Christian fundamentals.[80]

This is clearly seen in the "increase diversity"[81] among congregations, even within the same denomination. It is really great when one thinks of the body of Christ as unity among diversity. However, it becomes a problem within denominational lines because of the continuous struggle

---

78. Towns, *Is the Day of the Denomination Dead?*, 10–11, 50–51, 66–72.

79. Just to mention some historical factors, denominations at first were not considered as such, but most of today's protestant traditions go back to the time of the Reformation. The reformation would be the first example of how denominations emerged. Wagner says that when European state churches began to send missionaries they join together "in the receiving nation, and they began to take on the characteristics of denominations. The colonization and Christianization of America is an outstanding example." (Wagner, *Churchquake*, 19). The establishment in 1620 of the "separatists" colony who left the Anglican Church because they wanted to practice a congregational type of government is also an example (Vos, *Breve Historia de la Iglesia*, 120). A twentieth-century example is the establishment of the Assemblies of God in an effort to unite those who embraced Pentecostal teachings of speaking in tongues and divine healing and for which reason had been forced to break their own denominational ties (Blumhofer, "Assemblies of God," 23–24).

80. Ibid., 51–56.

81. Gibbs, *ChurchNext*, 67.

to keep "churches together in the face of diversity, verbal warfare, and often vicious denominational politics."[82] This occurs even when denominational leaders celebrate diversity as a sign that brings strength because of contributions different churches make.

Yet, another factor is the questioning of authority. Lay people who see the way things are going among their denomination, with regards to finances, membership decline due to transfer or death, lack of expansion and growth, and lack of vision from the leadership among other things, are bringing serious doubts about the leadership they have trusted to professionals in the denomination.[83] After the Vietnam War distrust to "institutional authority" of different sorts became increasingly common. The boomer generation even developed the "me generation" concept as a reaction to distrust of authority structures. Today's generation reacts against hierarchical structures of authority, a type of authority, which is common among traditional denominations.[84]

There is a growing tendency to persuade denominational members to keep sending money to the offices. Bureaucracy will make the money go from office to office leaving a bit of money in each step of the way until it reaches the final destination, where the little that remains is sent to "a finance service needed by congregations."[85]

People within denominational congregations understand the fact that they are living in a new century. This leads to another factor of denominational decline, the lack of leadership towards change. Although denominational leaders see changes around them in every aspect of life, they tend to work in the past. They know that a change is overdue, however, they tend to perpetuate the working system of the past.[86]

Adding to the problem of denominational decline is also the increasing demand on the pastor's load. Megachurches are large not only because of a great leader, but also because of a pastoral team. However, many mainline denominational churches of average size still want their pastors

---

82. Campolo, *Can Mainline Denominations Make a Comeback?*, 157–58.
83. Schaller, *The New Reformation*, 33.
84. Gibbs, *ChurchNext*, 68.
85. Schaller, *The New Reformation*, 33; see also, Gibbs, *ChurchNext*, 66, 69.
86. Schaller, *The New Reformation*, 33.

to perform as a one-person pastoral team. Pulpit committees require the new pastor to do a pastoral job a pastoral team does in a megachurch.[87]

The Problem of the Wineskins

Lyle Schaller notes a similarity of what is happening in today's Christian world and the world of the 1500s, when the Protestant Reformation took place. He notes that institutional expressions were in need of change, or of a reform, and the signs were obvious. The questions that rose in the 1500s are similar to todays: Should change come from within or from the outside? Should the old wineskins be patched or do we need new ones?[88]

The problem of the wineskins is nothing entirely new, as we learn from Jesus' parable in Luke 5:36–39. The idea of this parable is to have new wineskins for the new wine; otherwise, the fermentation of the new wine in old wineskins would break the wineskins and spill the wine. However, as the last verse says, no one who drinks the old one wants to drink the new, because the old one is better. This is matter of cultural change.

In similar way, the problem of the wineskins is felt among the generational change in the denominational arena. One of the important factors is the "erosion of institutional loyalties." As Schaller notes, the post-World War II generation was loyal to brand names, which is not the case in today's generation, especially the baby boomer generation attending leading edge congregations. Early in the twentieth century, denominational affiliation was very clear and even distinguished by geographical location. The picture began to change by the 1950s when the means of transportation were available to more people, especially the car. The media also played an important role: the radio, newspapers, and the TV, among other things. This brought the denominational barriers low, letting people hear and learn about other churches. During those days, people born within a denomination would stay in that denomination. This is not the case of today's church members, for whom switching denominations is easier.[89]

Miller notes that the values (like the negative meaning of tradition) of the baby boomer generation are, among other things, important factors in the problem of the wineskins. They prefer personal involvement rather

---

87. Gibbs, *ChurchNext*, 69; Campolo, *Can Mainline Denominations Make a Comeback?*, 149.

88. Schaller, *The New Reformation*, 17–19.

89. Ibid., 48; Miller, *Reinventing American Protestantism*, 17; Wuthnow, *Christianity in the Twenty-First Century*, 24–25.

than trusting top executives; they like to do things on their own, rather than entrusting decisions to the "pastor or priest." Another one is the tendency "to be local in their interests" rather than the remote interests of the denomination's headquarters. They see denominations spending too much money on irrelevant issues and "issues outside of their own communities."[90]

Miller also notes that, the baby boomer generation in leading edge congregations, or new paradigm churches as he calls them, has a tendency towards "[a]nti-establishment." They seem to be hostile to institutions, rejecting the symbols of "organized religion," considering them as oppressive and false. However, it is the pyramid style of leadership that they reject; hence their rejection of denominationalism.[91] As Schaller calls it, "a dark and growing cloud . . . is over traditional hierarchical systems." Even though the business sector has changed in this respect, it is taking long for the denominational system to flatten the structure granting more authority to people, affected by decisions made in denominational headquarters far away.[92]

The Denominational Cycle

Towns, following Ernst Troelch's view of the sociological cycle of the church, says there are four stages in the church: these four stages consider the church from its beginnings to the denominational stage.

The first one is the sectarian stage. This is the stage where there is an increase in "attendance, offerings, and membership." The next stage is the institutional stage, when the church sets its distinctives and becomes more rational. The denomination stage is where several churches group together under a centralize leader to accomplish what they can't individually. The last sage is the deterioration stage, where the decay process begins by losing sight of the original goals of the church founders.[93]

It is the last stage of the cycle that churches in the last half of the twentieth century wanted to evade. They caught the denominational cycle and instead of closing the cycle they decided to renew and revitalized their vision in order to keep the original purpose of the church as the body of Christ alive.[94]

---

90. Miller, *Reinventing American Protestantism*, 17.

91. Ibid., 22

92. Schaller, *The New Reformation*, 33–34.

93. Towns, *Is the Day of the Denomination Dead?*, 98–99.

94. Oakley and Krug note the dynamics of organizational change, calling for a

Signs of Postdenominationalism

Wagner was among the first ones to coin the name for a movement he saw arising in the last two decades of the twentieth century. Although the term was rejected, mainly because of the idea of past failures of denominations, or because it pointed to the ineffectiveness of denominations, the signs of postdenominationalism are clear.[95]

One of the signs is the growing number of congregations started after the decline of mainline denominations, especially during the Jesus movement. Examples of this are Calvary Chapel of Costa Mesa, The Vineyard, and Hope Chapel in California. These and other congregations were born with a renewed vision to reach the outcast of society. These are not the only ones; there is also an increase in the number of seeker-sensitive churches as well as other independent churches "loosely associated in 'apostolic networks'" leading some observers to speculate, "that we are entering a postdenominational era."[96]

Another clear sign is the increased number of congregations getting their resources from a variety of suppliers. Many congregations find that their denominations are not fulfilling their needs in denominational resources, such as Sunday school curriculum, leadership development, teacher development, even hymnals, and—most of all—consultation services, as well as "training materials for new ministries."[97]

Yet, another clear sign is the little importance people show about denominational affiliation. In today's world, people tend to switch denominational affiliations easier than in the past, to the point that many even choose non-denominational churches. There is an increase in "interfaith or interdenominational switching" clearly marked by the lack of teaching denominational distinctives reflected in membership requirements.[98]

---

continuous renewal. Although written for business leadership audience, the renewal cycle is very similar. They note three phases: the entrepreneurial phase, the growth phase, and the crisis phase. The growth phase is crucial because it is the phase where habits are developed. It is a phase "based on rules, policies, and structure." This phase leads to the next one, the crisis phase, where decisions have to be made, either to renew and revitalize the vision or to start the declining phase. However, in order to be successful, a continuous renewal is necessary (Oakley and Krug, *Enlightened Leadership*, 25–41).

95. Towns, "Foreword," 9.
96. Miller, *Reinventing American Protestantism*, 19.
97. Schaller, *The New Reformation*, 33.
98. Ibid., 48–49; Wuthnow, *Christianity in the Twenty-First Century*, 25, 156.

However, one of the more clear signs is the tolerance among denominations. This is reflected in sermons preached, where pastors seldom refer to their denominational distinctives, to the point that instead of talking of ecumenism, people and ministers talk about cooperation among churches. Ecumenism tends to pull towards a more traditional form of cooperation, while cooperation among churches leads to community "without making ecumenism an issue." Denominationalism seems to be high only among administrators, those seeking career opportunities, and those where policy-making would affect them in a favorable way. It is only for these that denominationalism is seeing a revival.[99]

In today's postdenominationalism those differences that kept us apart are not there anymore. Churches see what they have in common and unite efforts with other churches of different denominations with the same goals and vision, forming theological homogenization. People are only interested in the vision of carrying God's mission. However, as previously mentioned, only some of the clergy and top officials are interested in denominationalism, but people attending churches are living in a postdenominational time.[100]

This is postdenominationalism, what comes after the denomination stage in the church's cycle. This is what the church is doing in order to keep the original purpose of the church, as the body of Christ, alive. It does not imply the end of denominations as we know them; rather it implies an "ecclesiological revolution," which emphasis lies on a "change of relationships." Pablo Deiros notes that new and emerging postdenominational congregations in Latin America not only are independent, but they are actually interdependent because they are linked to each other under a common purpose, and this is not exclusive of the Latin American Christianity.[101]

On the other hand, postdenominationalism is highly marked by the mutual cooperation between churches of different Christian practices. It is also seen in the fact that many churches are still affiliated to their denomination, however they can be considered as "postdenominational in the way they develop their ecclesiastical life."[102] These churches "have

99. Wuthnow, *Christianity in the Twenty-First Century*, 156.

100. Ibid., 25.

101. Deiros, *Protestantismo en América Latina*, 100–101. Wagner, "Those Amazing Postdenominational Churches," 1.

102. Deiros, *Protestantismo en América Latina*, 103; see also Wagner, "The New Paradigms of Today's Emerging Churches," 51.

shed the shackles of their traditionalism without forfeiting the enrichment of their heritage."[103]

One clear example of a postdenominational church remaining within a traditional historical denomination is Iglesia Evangélica Bautista del Centro (Evangelical Central Baptist Church), in Buenos Aires Argentina, where Pablo Deiros was the pastor at the time of this writing. Hong in his book, *Una Iglesia Posmoderna?* (A Postmodern Church?), describes this church as a model of a new missiological perspective for the future.[104]

Theology of the Kingdom

As part of the religious background of the 1980s and 1990s, setting the background for the emergence of NACs, there is also a new worldview that is affecting the way Christianity is practiced. One of these changes has to do with respect to the understanding of the kingdom of God.

Changes in the way to view theology are not new, they are the result of renewal of the church. Such is the case of the theological developments after the major outpourings of the Spirit during the twentieth century. The Pentecostal movement of the early part of the twentieth century gave way to a number of doctrines expressed in different movements. One of this is the Latter Rain movement, as a result of the neo-Pentecostal deliverance revival. A byproduct of the Latter Rain movement is the Restoration movement, also known as Latter Rain Restoration that took place mainly during the Charismatic renewal of the 1960s and 1970s.[105]

However, many of the prominent doctrines of these renewals have been carried out and modified in some way in contemporary movements. Moriarty, for example, considers that Kingdom Theology is a strong part of the New Charismatics, popularized by the emphasis on restoration of the church. Moriarty argues that the latest Christian developments (he calls them new charismatics) are nothing less than a revival of the restorationist doctrines. He says that the main emphasis of the new charismatics lies on the fact that they expect to establish the kingdom of God, and then the Lord will come. Even his argument for the name "new charismatics" is because charismatics have always been restorationist. But because their "teachings and practices have changed so dramatically that in order for us

---

103. Gibbs, *ChurchNext*, 72.
104. Hong, *Una Iglesia Posmoderna?*, 2001.
105. Moriarty, *The New Charismatics*, 44, 60.

to understand what is really going on in the charismatic world, we must see this movement as something new."[106]

On the other hand, I think it is important to note the fact that kingdom theology is not the same as theology of the kingdom. Kingdom Theology is that kind of restorationist view that believers will Christianize the world in preparation for the coming of the King. It is more a dominion theology rather than kingdom theology. Theology of the kingdom has to do with the understanding of the kingdom of God; the church as a result of the kingdom and her mission in the power of the Spirit, and as the expression of the kingdom on earth.[107]

In the 1990s the theology of the kingdom was the result of a paradigm shift that is presently moving the church from "an institutional tradition to a theology of the kingdom."[108] In light of the recent developments, the church will need to move towards a global theology, which is expressed in the understanding of the kingdom of God taking precedence over the little kingdoms built around traditional denominations. This implies that the church goes from being a mere institution to being a true expression of the kingdom, focusing her mission on a more relevant and efficient way of doing ministry that will produce amazing results.[109]

The kingdom of God was central in Jesus' ministry; it means, "abolishing the kingdom of Satan."[110] As a central part of his work, Jesus referred to the kingdom of God in terms of his ministry, which in turn will be carried out by his disciples. At first, the idea was that the kingdom was confined to Israel; however, we also see that Jesus broke all kinds of barriers (see John 4 for example) implying that salvation is for all peoples.

---

106. Ibid., xiii.

107. Ibid., 160–61; Padilla, *Mission between the Times*, 191.

108. Deiros, *Protestantismo en América Latina*, 98–99.

109. The recent developments I'm referring to are the charismatic developments I dealt with in the preceding pages. When I say little kingdoms I'm referring mostly to the result of denominationalism, which was focused more on building the organization, rather than building the organism called church. Postdenominationalism is a result of the theology of the kingdom, as a different understanding as well as a reaction to the unfruitful efforts of denominations in church growth. Wagner asked some leaders of what he then called "post-denominational churches" about the rapid growth. The answers were centered in the idea of sufficient autonomy to "lead as God directs" as oppose to the "controls more common in denominational spheres," (Wagner, "The New Paradigms of Today's Emerging Churches," 52).

110. Boyd, *God at War*, 184–86.

Therefore in speaking of the kingdom of God, we must understand that it refers to the redemptive purpose of God that includes all of creation, being then, the mission of the church, that of bringing the redemptive purpose of God in "between the times," to all peoples of the earth, and as a result, the mission of the church itself, is the "extension of the mission of Jesus."[111]

Thus, the idea of the theology of the kingdom is that understanding that the kingdom of God takes precedence over institutional agendas. Churches of this paradigm[112] are more interested in the welfare of the kingdom rather than building their own kingdoms, or denominational purposes. The emphasis then falls, on joining God in his agenda, "rather than pursuing institutional agendas . . . these efforts will take us into the community and the world beyond the church walls."[113] When the local congregation understands the kingdom of God beyond the institutional or denominational barriers, then they develop a global vision to reach the community, the city, and the world (Acts 1:8). This global vision brings the unity of the church.

Unity of the Church

Unity of the church is also one of the later developments of the 1990s. Unity of the church is an effect of postdenominationalism. As churches break the denominational and doctrinal barriers, they begin to enter the postdenominational stage, and new wineskins are created for the new wine, that is the local congregation that understands the need for unity in order to accomplish its mission. This implies the use of everyone's "particular tradition, but without the barriers to separate us."[114]

According to Moriarty, the restoration efforts of the new charismatics are to bring down the barriers that divide the church in order for the saints to take dominion over the earth and establish God's kingdom. Therefore,

---

111. Castro, *Sent Free*, ix, 68–69; Padilla, *Mission between the Times*, 186, 192.

112. Deiros considers that the present state of the Church deserves to be called "new apostolic paradigm (Deiros, "The Roots and Fruits of the Argentine Revival," 49). Miller calls the churches that are revolutionizing American Protestantism as "New Paradigm Churches" (Miller, *Reinventing American Protestantism*, 1).

113. "Present Futures of the Church," www.ntcumc.org/ArcMyC/MyC9805.html.

114. Mraida, "Unity as a Sign of Revival," 191–92.

new charismatics assert the idea that a "common spiritual parentage and that unity of heart must take precedence over unity of doctrine."[115]

Ed Delph, in his article "Unleashing God's Power in Your City," talks about how his personal experience at a Carlos Annacondia crusade in Argentina in 1988 changed his view of the unity of the church. Annacondia explained to him the need for city pastors to give up their independence and proclaim "interdependence." This is not losing identity, but rather entering into mutual relationship with each other for the sake of the lost.[116]

The idea of the unity of the church is not an Argentinean one, but it is held by pastors of different countries too. Pastor Peter McHugh in Australia talks about the church he leads as "a congregation of the church in Melbourne." This brings up the idea of the church of the City. This idea of the church of the city is the New Testament vision of God for the city.[117] Several New Testament references attest to this, for example Acts 8:1; 1 Corinthians 1:2; 1 Thessalonians 1:1, where the reference is to the church of that specific city. One thing must be clear, and that is that the church of the city does not imply the abolishment of denominations, nor of a "local 'superchurch.'" However, the emphasis lies on the idea of many congregations and their own traditions, Christian convictions and diverse characteristics, unite efforts, and "share resources, leadership and forces" towards a common goal—to fulfill God's vision for the city.[118]

Delph uses the illustration of the Persian Gulf War, when several nations joined forces to "rescue Kuwait from Iraq." The joint armed forces of the nation left the established boundaries to join forces centered on a common goal. In similar way, "God is moving churches and pastors from a boundary-set to a center-set perspective."[119] However, unity is not the end, but the means to an end—and that is that the world believe in Jesus (John 17:23).

In church interrelationships, blessings are shared by all included in the relationships. The interdependence of churches is what makes the

---

115. Moriarty, *The New Charismatics*, 91; Hong, *Una Iglesia Posmoderna?*, 33.
116. Delph, "Unleashing God's Power in Your City," 27.
117. Ibid., 28.
118. Mraida, "Unity as a Sign of Revival," 186–87.
119. Delph, "Unleashing God's Power in Your City," 28.

church of the city strong to accomplish its mission.[120] And the most important thing to keep in mind is that when Christ comes back for his church, he will come for one church, not for a harem.[121]

Unity, therefore, does not mean uniformity. Unity of the church is when local congregations unite efforts to accomplish the mission of God. Churches will focus on a common goal in order to reach a common vision, using different forms. The focal point of the church must always be the church's mission. As long as churches have that focus in mind and are committed entirely to accomplish the "redemptive purposes of God in Christ," churches will soon understand that the enemy is Satan and his kingdom, and not other congregations.[122]

Effects of Communications in the 1990s

Although the information age did not begin in the 1980s or 1990s, it was during these years that it gained prominence. The advances in technology during these years are what made communications more accessible, breaking the information float. Time between communications is faster today than it was in the 1970s. Cable television, satellites, and computer technologies have also been important factors in communications during these years making communications more productive.[123]

Communications in the 1990s have brought the world closer. In today's world of communications, even the most remote towns and villages in the world are aware of what is happening in other parts of the planet. This has its effects especially in breaking down "regional boundaries" making people aware of each other. This at the same time brings up in people a consciousness about other religions in the world, which help people of different ages and cultures to see the richness of diversity there is. Taking this into consideration, religion and communications are compatible, even though many consider that media is for entertainment and religion is for regulating media and promoting moral and spiritual values.[124] The role of communications in missiology is very important, because missiologists become aware of unreached peoples, as well as the

---

120. Ibid., 29.
121. Ibid., 30; Deiros, "The Roots and Fruits of the Argentine Revival," 50.
122. Mraida, "Unity as a Sign of Revival," 189–91.
123. Naisbitt, *Megatrends*, 1–4, 14–16.
124. Arthur, *The Globalization of Communications*, 4, 14, 36.

accessibility with regards to them, in order to develop a strategy to reach them with the gospel of Christ.

Another of the important effects of communications in the 1990s is the fact that the information explosion during this decade has helped in breaking down the denominational barriers. With access to other people of different cultures and denominational backgrounds, via the Internet or satellite TV for example, help people to know each other better, as well as to find out what they have in common making whatever differences minimal. Thus, what people have in common becomes more important than what distinguish each other. With technological advances in years to come, this will increase, helping in the process of postdenominationalism.[125]

There is also an increment on relationships enhancing the networking revolution of the 1980s. Networking was the byproduct of a reaction "against" institutionalism, when institutions failed to fulfill people's needs.[126] In the 1990s, the accessibility to the Internet made possible a faster dissemination of information, flattening in this way the organizational structures. Through cyberspace, people have the ability to promote their ideas, many of them reactionary to the institutionalism of religious organizations, to the point of threatening many traditional institutions.[127]

Emergence of New Apostolic Churches

This section of the study has shown the religious backgrounds of the 1980s, with special emphasis on the 1990s. The emergence of New Apostolic Churches has been traced from a historical perspective, having as a background the different charismatic developments after the Charismatic movement of the 1960s. Although New Apostolic Churches were not recognized or named as such until the publication of Wagner's book *The New Apostolic Churches*, these churches trace their roots back three or four decades.

125. Deiros, *Protestantismo en América Latina*, 115. People from different denominations, with access to the Internet, talk to each other many times exchanging their Christian experiences. Those believers find out that what they are living in their cities, states or countries, is the same as what is happening in other parts of the world, in different denominations, from historical traditional denominations to the independent charismatic and the New Apostolic Churches. This awareness awakes a sense of a global spiritual revival taking place at the same time in the world.

126. Naisbitt, *Megatrends*, 219.

127. See Tom Beaudoin on the implications of the cyberspace revolution as cited in Gibbs, *ChurchNext*, 83–84.

A wider picture, starting from the beginnings of the Pentecostal movement, will show how the New Apostolic Churches emerged from recent charismatic developments. The outpouring of the Holy Spirit in early 1901 and 1906 gave birth to the Pentecostal movement. A second outburst of the outpouring of the Holy Spirit reached the historical denominations, giving birth to the Charismatic movement of the 1960s. Later on, in the 1980s, a third outpouring gives birth to the Third Wave of the Holy Spirit. In the meantime, some churches confronting opposition from their denomination, and not wanting to associate themselves with the classical Pentecostals, become independent, giving birth to the Independent Charismatic movement.

The Third Wave and the Independent Charismatic movement gives birth to what is called the Neo-Charismatics. This new movement, although not completely new, considers that the Charismatic movement of the 1960s is over, and that God is doing a new work among the church.

The combination of the latest three movements, the Third Wave, the Independent Charismatics, and The Neo-Charismatics opens the door to the postdenominational era giving birth to the postdenominational church. However, this name did not become popular, especially among denominational leaders, who reacted against it, until Wagner finally settle for the name New Apostolic Churches.

Figure 1 serves as a way to illustrate the historical emergence of New Apostolic Churches. The following chapter in this study will focus on the events that mark the emergence of the New Apostolic Churches.

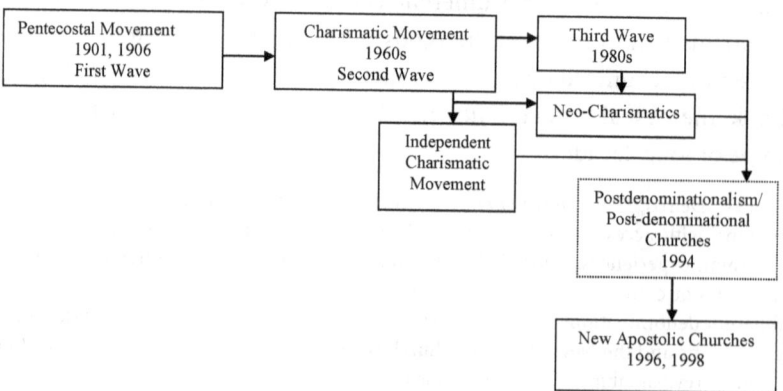

Figure 6. Charismatic Developments: A Timeline

6

The Emergence of New Apostolic Churches

THE SECULAR EVENTS AND trends as well as the religious background described in the previous chapter set the stage for the emergence of New Apostolic Churches (NACs). New Apostolic Churches were not born out of a vacuum; they are the result of cultural and sociological changes in society.

From the Protestant point of view, NACs are the result of charismatic developments rooted in the Pentecostal and Charismatic movements of the twentieth century. The Independent Charismatic movement was born after several charismatic leaders who were still within their denomination and were feeling strong opposition from their peers but did not want to be associated with classical Pentecostals decided to stay independent. Churches of this sort grew in membership as well as in outreach to other nations. Although many Independent Charismatic Churches separated from their denominations, many new congregations were born as independent.[1]

New independent churches already practicing the experiences of the Third Wave (signs and wonders) became known by others as "neo-charismatics." Later on, experiencing the solitude of being independent as well as experiencing the need to fellowship, they started to network with other churches of similar experiences "under prominent apostolic leaders."[2]

---

1. Poussson, *Spreading the Flame*, 39–40.
2. Moriarty, *The New Charismatics*, xiii; see also Pousson, *Spreading the Flame*, 28.

Many churchgoers, experiencing an emptiness in their historical denominations, and as a reaction to the lack of spiritual development, began to attend churches of the new style. The new style of being the church began to proliferate among many independent congregations in recent years, which has contributed to postdenominationalism, a reaction to "a general disillusionment with bureaucratic hierarchies and organizational oversight."[3] However, many other congregations have shifted to the new style or, to be more precise, to a new paradigm, while remaining in their original denomination, but practicing different forms of "worship and organizational style" than is typical of the more institutionalized churches. Therefore, these churches, whatever their ecclesiological distinctive, can be considered as NACs because of their focus and attitude.[4]

Miller considers this trend a revolution in American Protestantism, to the point of being "viewed as the initial phase of a 'Second Reformation.'" It is a revolution that began with the Jesus movement of the 1960s as an effect of the cultural changes of the time, but that today NACs cannot be considered to represent the countercultural values of the time, as the Jesus movement churches did. However, NACs reflect the cultural transformations by the fact that they are filled with baby boomers and baby busters reflecting their values.[5]

CATALYST OF THE NACS

A catalyst is something or someone that helps produce change. It is an agent of change.[6] It is in this regard that I will consider Lyle E. Schaller, Donald Miller and especially, C. Peter Wagner: because of their contribution, they are agents of change in the process towards a better understanding of the NACs, but most of all, to recognize the reality of their existence as well as the reality that a new paradigm in the history of the church-in-mission is already in progress. Although these authors have written extensively in their individual careers, I will focus this section to examine their contribution about NACs.

---

3. Miller, *Reinventing American Protestantism*, 1.
4. Deiros, *Protestantismo en América Latina*, 116.
5. Miller, *Reinventing American Protestantism*, 1, 12.
6. "Catalyst," in *Encarta Encyclopedia*.

The Role of Lyle E. Schaller

Schaller is "considered to be America's leading church consultant" to the point that some think of him "as the dean of church consultants." Schaller considers himself to be "a loyal denominationalist."[7]

In 1994, Schaller was a prominent figure of the "Leadership Network" summit that met under the title "The Future of Denominations." In this meeting, Schaller brought out a key question of the meeting: he asked if there was a future for denominations. His response was that denominations have the final answer, the willingness to change and adapt to a new paradigm.[8]

One of Schaller's most important contributions towards understanding NACs as well as to realizing the new era in the history of the church in mission is his book *The New Reformation: Tomorrow Arrived Yesterday* (1995). In this book Schaller calls the reader's attention to what is going on in American Christianity. Schaller boldly calls it "a new reformation." It is a wake-up call to see that many ministers and denominations are ministering in the past and expecting a future that is already here.

Schaller presents twenty-one signs of the new reformation in the last chapter of his book and considers that the new reformation is in its early stages. Some of these signs are: "the arrival of a new era in Christian music; the change in public worship in thousands of Protestant churches; market-driven planning"; trust in the laity to minister; emergence of thousands of mega-churches; a shift in the building blocks towards ecumenism, from denominations to the pastor and the local church.[9] Schaller also explores the characteristics of the new reformation, implications for ministry in the new reformation, and the assumptions that led to a new reformation.

The Role of Donald Miller

Miller, Professor of Religion at the University of Southern California, has contributed in the understanding of the new paradigm and the churches of the new paradigm. Miller, feeling somewhat frustrated after his graduate studies in theology, decided to join a liberal Episcopal church, that was more interested in social justice than in "purity of doctrine." He knew

---

7. Wagner, *Churchquak*, 28; Schaller, *The New Reformation*, back cover.
8. Wagner, *Churchquake*, 28.
9. Schaller, *The New Reformation*, 13.

that the institution of religion was based on social construction; however, there was something else that gave meaning "to the lives of individuals." Nevertheless, Miller decided to put aside his quest in a way of escaping the intellectual challenge.

A decade later, as a teacher of sociology of religion on undergraduate level, he noticed what some of his students were reporting in their term papers—a phenomenon was happening in some Christian churches and church services were being conducted in an unconventional way. After attending some of these churches and finding out that there was something there worth researching, Miller requested funding from the Lilly Endowment for a research project.

Miller soon found out that these churches were practicing some New Testament–like Christianity. People were being healed and casting out of demons. Although he did not agree with all of their teachings, he could not deny the fact that the churches he researched had "connected with the spirit of 'Christianity' in ways" that his colleagues would have missed or feared.

Miller reported his findings in the book *Reinventing American Protestantism: Christianity in the New Millennium* (1997). Miller says that even though it would be easy to criticize the churches of the study, it is not his intention to do so. His intentions are to show the many "ways in which they are responding to the major cultural crises of our time" and "the religious and cultural significance of these groups."[10]

In his book Miller does a study of The Vineyard, Calvary Chapel, and Hope Chapel. Miller considers these churches as prototypes of what he calls "new paradigm churches."[11] He also speaks of a revolution taking place in American Protestantism that is leading to the formation of new congregations that respond to cultural changes already in place.

The Role of C. Peter Wagner

Wagner is probably the one author and researcher that has contributed the most to the understanding of New Apostolic Churches and the recent developments in church growth. As a researcher, Wagner recognizes three main seasons of research dealing with specific aspects of church growth. His research has been presented through classes developed for

---

10. Miller, *Reinventing American Protestantism*, 6–9.
11. Ibid., 1–3.

graduate level students at Fuller Theological Seminary, which eventually became books.¹²

Wagner was not born in a Christian home. His formation was classically evangelical and he studied under Wilbur Smith, Harold Lindsell, and Carl Henry at Fuller Seminary, and he was ordained "in a Bible Church associated with F.I.C.A." Wagner and his wife served as missionaries in Bolivia for sixteen years with the South American Indian Mission and the Andes Evangelical Mission. Because of his background, Wagner had "a strong aversion to liberals of any kind," and was also anti-Pentecostal.¹³

Wagner considers that during his missionary term in Bolivia he was a "missionary without power." Accepting the missionary call like the Apostle Paul, Wagner clearly understood the Great Commission as well as the biblical foundation of power for mission. However, in looking back at this time, Wagner says, "I cannot recall that kind of power ever operating in my ministry. I never cast out an evil spirit. I never healed a sick person."¹⁴

Wagner began the paradigm shift at Fuller Seminary studying under Donald McGavran. Wagner's first season was when he decided to study the churches that were growing the fastest, which happened to be the Pentecostal churches. It was during the 1970s that the paradigm shift began to occur.¹⁵

The next season of study for Wagner was the season of Signs and Wonders (The Third Wave of the Holy Spirit) during the 1980s. During this time, Wagner began to work with John Wimber. It was also during these years that Wimber planted a new congregation, The Anaheim Vineyard. While teaching church growth at Fuller Seminary in conjunction with Wimber, they first introduced the subject of signs and wonders to the faculty, and the Dean of the School of World Mission (then Paul Pierson). Pierson approved the class "MC510 Signs, Wonders and Church Growth" to be scheduled for 1982.¹⁶

During the season of Signs and Wonders, Wagner began the third season: research, prayer and spiritual warfare (1987–1996). This led

12. Wagner, "The New Apostolic Reformation," 14.
13. Wagner, "Contemporary Dynamics of the Holy Spirit in Missions," 3.
14. Wagner, *The Third Wave of the Holy Spirit*, 19–20.
15. Wagner, "Contemporary Dynamics of the Holy Spirit in Missions," 4; *The Third Wave of the Holy Spirit*, 22–23.
16. Ibid., 5–6; *The Third Wave of the Holy Spirit*, 15–24.

Wagner to the leadership of the International Warfare Network, which later united into the "AD2000 United Prayer Track" becoming a "Prayer Track Coordinator."[17]

All of the background studies collected until this time helped Wagner to see a phenomenon taking place in churches around the world. In 1993, Wagner began to study some churches that were rapidly growing and which did "not fit into traditional categories or classifications."[18] It was a "radical change in the way of doing church in world Christianity since the Protestant Reformation," says Wagner. The most intriguing thing about these churches was the fact that many missiologists were studying them, but they had not agreed upon a name for such a movement. Wagner saw that these congregations combined every technical aspect he had studied about church growth.[19]

Wagner's most important contribution is probably the naming of these churches. He first named these churches "post-denominational." In 1994, Wagner writes an article for *Ministries Today* (July/August issue) entitled "Those Amazing Postdenominational Churches." In this first article on the subject, Wagner presents some examples, defines the new style, and for the first time, gives the main characteristics of the churches.

Early in 1996 Wagner conceived the idea of a movement, one he called "Postdenominational Movement." However, this name brought some protest from denominational leaders, which led Wagner to experiment with different names, finally settling for "New Apostolic Reformation, and individual churches being designated as new apostolic churches."[20]

Although postdenominational churches "traced their roots back three or four decades," it was only in the 1990s that these churches "gained a high enough profile to attract widespread notice." To give the movement a wider recognition, Fuller Theological Seminary convened a symposium on the postdenominational church to be held in May 21–23, 1996. It was advertised as the "first National Symposium on the Postdenominational Church," featuring more than forty speakers with

17. Wagner, "Contemporary Dynamics of the Holy Spirit in Missions," 6–8.

18. Wagner, "Those Amazing Postdenominational Churches," 1.

19. Wagner, "Those Amazing Postdenominational Churches," 1; "Contemporary Dynamics of the Holy Spirit in Missions," 9.

20. Wagner, "The New Paradigms of Today's Emerging Churches." 51; "The New Apostolic Reformation," 18.

eleven panels. All those who attended the symposium were given the recently published book "The Gift of Apostle," dealing with the subject of present day apostles and the apostolic movement (later published as *Apostles and the Emerging Apostolic Movement*) by David Cannistraci, also a speaker at the symposium.[21]

In 1997, Fuller Seminary "approved a new course, MG545 Churches of the New Apostolic Paradigm." In this course, Wagner presented the historical roots of these churches in all six continents as well as the major characteristics of such churches. A year later, Wagner edited his first book presenting these new styles of churches, *The New Apostolic Churches* (1998). Wagner wrote the first chapter presenting the New Apostolic Reformation. The rest of the chapters were written by pastors and leaders of New Apostolic Churches and Networks, who gave their personal testimonies as well as the characteristics of the churches or movements they lead. In 1999, Wagner published *Churchquake!* In this book, Wagner deals with the New Apostolic Reformation in a more defined way. He presents the philosophy of the movement as well as expanding on the characteristics of the new apostolic churches.[22]

The Role of the Spiritual Warfare Movement

The main characteristic of the Third Wave is the emphasis on signs and wonders, which has to do with laying hands when praying for healing, or in many cases in prayers of deliverance from demonic forces. Wagner calls this "fourth-dimension faith," as the shield of faith described in Ephesians 6.[23]

As previously shown (see Figure 6), NACs were born after the Independent Charismatic movement, the Third Wave and the New Charismatics. However, the point of convergence among them is spiritual warfare. Spiritual warfare is characteristic of the three movements. Spiritual warfare emerges as a "specific ideology" in the 1980s, but gains prominence in the 1990s, becoming central in the teachings and practices

---

21. Wagner, "The New Paradigms of Today's Emerging Churches," 51; See also advertisement on *Ministries Today*, March/April 1996, 56.

22. Although the New Apostolic Reformation has not been widely recognized as a movement, it is considered as a movement because of the people, pastors, and church network leaders moving in the same direction and influencing one another by sharing a common goal.

23. Wagner, *The Third Wave of the Holy Spirit*, 41.

of NACs, due to the fact that NACs are also pragmatic, a common characteristic of the church Growth movement.[24]

The 1990s saw also a revival in praise and worship as part of the charismatic developments that help nurture postdenominational churches (NACs). The praise and worship movement goes along with spiritual warfare. As Moriarty points out, that the recent outpouring of the Holy Spirit has had its effects in "reestablishing anointed worship of Christ's church." This new anointing that flows from praise and worship endows believers with spiritual power to defeat God's enemies. The different manifestations while worship is conducted, such as clapping, dancing, singing and "proclaiming prophetic words," among others, are not only considered as part of the worship service, but as acts of spiritual warfare "against God's enemies."[25]

Spiritual warfare plays an important role in the emergence of NACs because of the paradigm shift experience. NACs are also denominational churches that have experienced a paradigm shift in their theology of mission, which includes spiritual warfare. NACs have understood their mission as the church of Jesus Christ. As the body of Christ, NACs see themselves as the continuation of Jesus' ministry, which is "setting up God's rule where previously there had been Satan's rule." Both concepts of the "Kingdom of God and the kingdom of Satan are correlative," as Gregory Boyd says, and the expansion of the first one implies the diminishing of the second one.[26]

NACs have come to the understanding that in order to expand the Kingdom of God, they have to enter into spiritual warfare, taking in this way an active and offensive position against the powers of evil. The spiritual warfare movement has played an important role in helping NACs realize that the body of Christ has been given authority to minister healing and to set people free. It is a realization of being the body of Christ; the extension of Jesus' ministry, which is to "breakdown Satanic fortresses"[27] in an aggressive way in order to expand the kingdom. This is what the church's ministry is about.[28]

---

24. Hong, *Una Iglesia Posmoderna?*, 36.
25. Moriarty, *The New Charismatics*, 103–4.
26. Boyd, *God at War*, 185.
27. Ibid., 217.
28. Bottari, "Dealing With Demons in Revival Evangelism," 81–82.

The Role of the Cell Group Movement

The cell group movement is a development of the late 1970s. Korean Pastor Paul Yonggi Cho, was taken to the hospital after suffering a heart attack, and during his stay God led him through several passages of Scripture, showing him a strategy for the growth of the church and for people's development in ministry. In 1976 Cho founded the "International Organization for Church Growth with the purpose of bringing to the pastors and lay leaders of the world, the message and knowledge of the principles of the growth of the Church."[29]

From the late 1970s, cell group evangelism has become a worldwide phenomenon. Several churches around the world are rapidly growing because they are employing cell group dynamics. Cell group dynamics not only include evangelism and discipleship, but leadership development as well. This is a paradigm shift in the way churches conduct their ministry. It is a church where the cell is the more basic form of life.[30]

Cell group ministry is central in the core values of NACs. NACs aim toward felt needs of people, which can only be met in a family environment, provided by cell groups. People tend to see the cell group meeting their spiritual needs better than the large meeting celebration on Sundays. Besides, non-Christians will tend to see more of the believer's actions rather than listening to what they have to say. People also find support for each other in times of trouble, as well as a means of accountability for personal behavior through their cell group.[31]

Although many NACs tend to be mega-churches, they develop their ministry through cell groups.[32] It is through cell groups that NACs can develop practical ministry, through the development of the ministry of all believers. In this way, NACs are living out their expectations to be the church in the twenty-first century, which mirrors as closely as possible the first century church—that is, the Apostolic Paradigm.

In *The New Apostolic Churches* (1998), several NAC leaders give their personal testimony as well as how they develop their ministry. The book serves to present the New Apostolic Reformation and a sample of churches considered as NACs. In it several of the leaders show how cell

---

29. Cho, *Los Grupos Familiares y el Crecimiento de la Iglesia*, 1–31.
30. Comiskey, *Home Cell Group Explosion*, 15–19.
31. Ibid., 81; Miller, *Reinventing American Protestantism*, 137.
32. Wagner, "The New Paradigms of Today's Emerging Churches," 51.

group ministry is central to the churches they lead and to the planting and growing of new congregations.[33]

Cell group ministry is devoted to evangelism and multiplication. Evangelism brings non-Christians to faith and, through the cell group, people begin a journey of training and spiritual development towards the leadership of a cell. In the cell group people receive pastoral care and instruction in the faith as well as practical and theory training in cell ministry. Passion for souls is the driving force of the cells that keeps them moving and growing.[34]

Typically, a cell group will grow and multiply within six months. Multiplication is that time when a new cell is born out of an existing one. Cell groups that have sprung from one mother cell will see the original cell group leader as their mentor/pastor, a person who supervises the cell group leader's personal and ministry development. Usually, these cells grow into new congregations that trace their spiritual link to the mother church.[35] It is in this way that a church plant movement begins, many times developing into an apostolic ministry, which is characteristic of the NACs.

The Role of Mega-churches—From Mega-church to NAC

Wagner notes that the largest churches in "almost any metropolitan area" are usually NACs. Some examples of this are: Deeper Life Bible Church in Lagos, Nigeria with an attendance of seventy-four thousand adults on a given Sunday; Waves of Love and Peace Church of Buenos Aires, Argentina, in less than ten years has grown to one hundred and fifty thousand people in membership; and New Life Church of Colorado Springs, Colorado in the United States counts four thousand people at worship.[36]

As stated in the previous section, cell groups are at the core of NACs. Cells are the basic structure of NACs because they help people in personal as well as ministry development. Cells are expected to multiply and to eventually become new church plants. Many of the mega-churches of the world are cell-based churches, otherwise it would be impossible for

---

33. Wagner, *The New Apostolic Churches*, 81–82, 105–6, 165–68, 217–20.
34. For further understanding of cell group ministry see Comiskey, *Home Cell Group Explosion*.
35. Ibid., Miller, *Reinventing American Protestantism*, 15, 137.
36. Wagner, "Those Amazing Postdenominational Churches," 1.

pastors to care for such a large group. Besides, the role of the ministry of all believers is reclaimed by NACs, leaving the pastor of the church with the responsibility of casting the vision and leading the general direction of the church. An example of this is Calvary Chapel of Costa Mesa, California, led by Chuck Smith. As the founding pastor Chuck Smith has given lay ministry an important role. Smith holds staff meetings only twice a year, in which many times his position is to approve or disapprove plans; but pastors have full autonomy because he believes that "ministry is between staff members and the Holy Spirit."[37]

NACs are not a new denomination; however, they are a renewed way of being the church. Churches considered as new apostolic are those which, after going through a paradigm shift, understand their mission in light of the New Testament church that accepted the fivefold ministry as presented in Ephesians 4:11.

Cannistraci defines an apostolic church as that church which recognizes and relates to present-day apostles as well as develops an apostolic ministry. Cannistraci says that the work of an apostle, among other things, is that of planting new churches and overseeing the growth of those churches. They also develop leaders and help them in times of crisis.[38]

Mega-churches become NACs when they begin to develop an apostolic ministry. Cell group strategy is a vehicle towards apostolic ministry, because of the development and nurture of leaders. An example of a mega-church becoming an NAC is the International Charismatic Mission (ICM) of Bogotá, Colombia, led by pastor Cesar Castellanos. Castellanos had a dramatic conversion experience after reading the Book of Genesis, ending up in God reveling himself to him. Castellanos soon began to preach on the streets of Bogotá, and for several years pastored different churches of different denominations. In 1983, Castellanos received a vision from the Lord that encouraged him to start a new congregation, this time in his living room. Castellanos named the new church International Charismatic Mission, which in three months grew to two hundred people.

In 1986, Cesar and his wife Claudia visited Cho's church in Korea, and came away with a transformed vision of unlimited growth. After implementing the cell system, the church grew to seventy cells in seven years. By 1991, frustrated by the small growth, Castellanos prayed to the

---

37. Miller, *Reinventing American Protestantism*, 139.
38. Cannistraci, *Apostles and the Emerging Apostolic Movement*, 28, 95–104.

Lord, and after examining the Scriptures received a "revelation of the 12." Sometime later, Castellanos began to develop the G–12 system of cell groups, understanding that Jesus centered his attention upon his twelve, and from 1991 to 1994, ICM grew to 1,200 cells. But the most dramatic growth was during 1995–1999 when the church grew from 4,000 to 10,500 cells and to 20,000 by 1999 with a regular attendance of 45,000 people at the Sunday celebration "in the indoor stadium and the satellite churches throughout Bogotá." Important within ICM core values is "authority and submission" which is reflected in the way people at ICM willingly submit to Cesar Castellanos, "who is considered an apostle."[39]

Other examples are presented in *The New Apostolic Churches* (1998). Such examples as: Willow Creek Community Church in South Barrington, Illinois, Victory Christian Center of Tulsa, Oklahoma, and Faith Community Baptist Church of Singapore.

GLOBAL CHARACTER OF NACS

In the previous sections I dealt with the events that mark the origins of New Apostolic Churches (NACs). One of the important factors in studying these churches was the concern of missiologists about the rapid growth rates of NACs as well as their places of ministry, ranging from the United States to Latin America, to Asia and Africa, namely, over the six continents.[40]

Churches of this sort were rapidly growing in different parts of the world, many times without any connection between them. However, what it was clear there was a commonality in the way they understood their mission as well as the renewed spirit with which they embarked in ministry. From a missiological perspective, the question is what are the implications of such a phenomenon? Are these the signs of a global renewal in the mission of the church? If so, is this a global phenomenon?[41]

In an era of globalization, the global character of NACs is not impossible to conceive, nor is the idea of networking among NACs, reaching the UNITED STATES and other parts of the world. What one can see is

---

39. Comiskey, *Groups of 12*, 22–25, 33; Castellanos *Sueña y Ganarás al Mundo*, 84–85, 109–10.

40. Wagner, "Those Amazing Postdenominational Churches," 1; "The New Paradigms of Today's Emerging Churches," 51; "The New Apostolic Reformation," 17.

41. Deiros, "From Renewal to Revival," 7.

"God's work from a globalized perspective."[42] Deiros notes several indicators of such work. Among them are: a different missionary consciousness, especially among the Majority World countries; the urbanization of the church, this is a renewing of the mind to an urban mentality, to the point that many large congregations are urban; the increase in the cell group strategy; an awakening of the Spiritual gifts as well as ministries of all the people of God; development of church plant movements under apostolic figures; the recognition of present day apostles leading church networks; a revival in praise and worship; and an increase of unity among the churches of different denominations.[43]

As a worldwide phenomenon, NACs are not a global denomination, but they are the work of God, a work that was perceived by missiologists in the last two decades of the twentieth century. However, as previously stated, NACs trace their roots two or three decades before. What is happening is a major missiological paradigm shift taking place. It is a paradigm shift of global proportions, about the understanding of the church itself and of her mission in the world.

NACs' Origins in Majority World Countries

Although NACs are rapidly proliferating in the United States, NACs are not made in the USA. Many NACs are national in their origin, especially among Majority World countries. Wagner says that in 1993 he began to see a phenomenon taking place in churches of three different continents. He then began to tie bits and pieces of information collected through his years as professional church growth expert. Wagner saw a trend among the African Independent Churches, the Chinese house churches and the Grassroots churches of Latin America.[44]

In Africa, the independent church movement began with churches started "in the late 1800s or early 1900s," and not initiated by European or American missionaries, but originated from the people. These are the African-Initiated Churches (AICs). Among these are the New Independent Churches (NICs), which are part of the South African charismatic movement. These churches "grew out of the Charismatic movement of the 1960s" as a result of church splits or, in many cases, began

---

42. http://www.cephasministry.com/apostles_new_church.html
43. Deiros, "From Renewal to Revival," 8.
44. Wagner, "The New Apostolic Reformation," 17.

as home Bible studies. These churches show variants in doctrine, core values, as well as people composition and political views. They are centered in local contexts, however, because of their "vision and creativity, these churches are always also transnational, international, or global."[45] The African Independent Churches (AICs and NICs) are experiencing rapid growth, exceeding that of the traditional denominations.[46]

In Asia, the house churches of China are another example of NACs experiencing rapid growth. This has been a missiological phenomenon in the last few decades. Prior statistics said that China had only 5 percent of its population confessing Christ as personal Savior. With the rapid growth of the house church movement, "Chinese evangelicals constitute between 20 to 25% of the world."[47] In Thailand, the Hope of God International, a church planting movement led by Kriensgak Chaeronwongsak, who holds a PhD degree and teaches economics at the university, had planted a total of 366 churches in Thailand by 1996, and thirty churches in sixteen other nations.[48]

In Latin America, many of the largest churches have been planted with no foreign missionary support, nor have the pastors had professional ministry training.[49] Mike Berg and Paul Pretiz[50] call this "Grassroots Protestantism" or "The Fifth Wave."[51] These churches have certain characteristics: the music they use for worship goes with what is in tune among the people, hymnals have been changed for new songs sung to a Latin beat; churches begin when a person in the community experience conversion in a dramatically way, and then opens his/her house to start a Bible study. When people begin to crowd the living room, they move to the outside patio or begin to remodel the house to accommodate the growth. When

45. Hexham and Poewe, "Charismatic Churches in South Africa," 58–59.
46. Wagner, "The New Apostolic Reformation," 17.
47. Deiros, *Protestantismo en América Latina*, 87.
48. Wagner, "Contemporary Dynamics of the Holy Spirit in Missions," 9.
49. Wagner, "The New Apostolic Reformation," 17.
50. Berg and Pretiz, *The Gospel People*.
51. The term "Fifth Wave," used by Berg and Pretiz is to identify the different aspects of Latin American Protestantism since the arrival of the first missionaries. According to them, Latin America has experienced a changed in its outlook. From the initial forms of evangelization brought by the first missionaries, to the use of revival tents, to the new churches, the grassroots churches (Berg and Pretiz, *The Gospel People*, 117). Fifth Wave then, does not have anything to do with the naming of the outpouring of the Holy Spirit, commonly known as the Third Wave of the Holy Spirit.

people in these churches see that a nearby neighborhood does not have any kind of witness, they consider it as a white field, ready for harvest, and a new group starts. This new group then becomes a daughter church, following the same process, until many congregations begin to network together reaching the city.[52]

Although many NACs in Majority World Countries are considered as independent churches, because of the unusual naming, not bearing their denomination's name, or because of difficulty in recognizing of such style of ministry, NACs in majority world countries began as congregations with a different type of ministry. One example of this is Omar Cabrera's Vision of the Future Church in Argentina, which began in the 1970s. Other evangelicals rejected Cabrera's ministry at first, because of the innovative methods he used, as well as the then unusual, spiritual manifestations. However, after "acts of reconciliation have taken place," some now consider Cabrera "as the chief apostle of the Argentine revival."[53]

As an important example of the NACs in Majority World Countries, the Argentine revival is a major contributor of the renewal and revival taking place in America, bringing many denominational congregations to become NACs. What is happening is an increased "Pentecostalization"[54] of the church, which is greatly impacted and influenced by Pentecostal and Grassroots churches that are rapidly growing in Majority World Countries.[55]

NACs Impact in the United States

The impact of NACs in the United States is two-fold. On the one hand there are those who consider a need for NACs, because of the benefits of this kind of being the church. On the other, of course is the opposite. This side considers that NACs are a threat to the church. Proponents of this

---

52. Ibid., 117.
53. Wagner, "Revival Power: God Has Set His People 'A-Praying,'" 20.
54. Pentecostalization does not have a denominational meaning. Pentecostalization is used in the sense of the tendency towards a personal experience with the Holy Spirit, as well as with the increase emphasis on the importance of a personal experience with God, as oppose to a rationalization of God (Deiros, *Protestantismo en América Latina*, 120–22).
55. Deiros, *Protestantismo en América Latina*, 122; "The Roots and Fruits of the Argentine Revival," 39.

view consider the emerging New Apostolic Churches and movement as preliminary to "the structure and government of a World Church."[56]

According to Tricia Tillin and Orrel Steinkamp, the "New Apostolic Reformation is nothing more than warmed-over Latter Rain teaching." They argue that Wagner and other church leaders are meeting to develop new doctrines and new structures for the "NEW global church," and denominations as we know them are considered obsolete. Tillin says that doctrine is not important, but renewal and revival as well as spiritual manifestations are taking precedence over biblical doctrines in the New Apostolic Church. She goes on to say that for some years C. Peter Wagner and other leaders from different organizations, such as AD 2000 and Promise Keepers, have been meeting in Colorado Springs, "to create a Centre for World Christianity—a Vatican City of the new church."[57]

On the other hand, Ebbie Smith of Southwest Baptist Theological Seminary, in his article "The New Apostolic Church: Fad, Impractical, or Imperative?" argues in favor of new apostolic churches. Smith considers the new apostolic church that which is concentrated in the needs of the unchurched, with special focus on how to reach them. Smith says that NACs are needed in the United States for several reasons. One of these is that "present-day evangelism has failed to meet the need." Smith points out the fact that 50 percent of the United States population is unchurched, as well as there being plateau and growth decline.[58]

Another important factor is worldview change in the United States and the churches' lack of change in their worldview. There is also the change from modernity to postmodernity, affecting the church. Postmodernism with secularism and its emphasis on materialism leaves no room for God, as well as the emergence of postmodern spirituality, expressed through new age groups, neo-paganism and Eastern spirituality. Smith argues that these are imperatives that should move the church to apostolic ministry, and that NACs are the ones that find ways to target

---

56. Tillin and Steinkamp, "The Second Pentecost Leads to the World Church," http://www.members.ozemail.com.au/~rseaborn/apostles.html. Accessed April 13 and July 5, 2001.

57. Ibid. Accessed April 13, 2001.

58. Smit, "*The New Apostolic Church,*" http://www.swbts.edu/si/articles/apostolichrch.htm.

and reach these kinds of people, tailoring "approaches that fit their particular questions and lifestyles."⁵⁹

NACs in Majority World Countries have had an impact in the United States also. An example of this is pastor Larry Stockstill, of the Bethany World Prayer Center in Bethany, Louisiana. Stockstill first visited the International Charismatic Mission of Colombia in 1996 to learn about the G-12 cell principle implemented by Cesar Castellanos. Since this first visit, Stockstill has been teaching in his yearly conferences about this principle.⁶⁰

Another example is the impact of the Argentine revival of the 1980s in churches, not only in America, but also in Europe—especially in England. The Toronto, Canada and Pensacola, Florida revivals are examples of this sort of revival tracing, in some way, their roots to the Argentine revival. John Arnott of the Toronto Airport Vineyard first went to Argentina desperately seeking a fresh touch of the Holy Spirit. When he heard of Ed Silvoso's trips to Argentina, he signed up and received a new anointing at Claudio Freidzon's King of Kings church. Once the new touch of the Holy Spirit came to the Toronto Airport Vineyard, many came from different parts of the world, among them "Eleanor Mumford of the South West London Vineyard" who was also touched.⁶¹

The Pensacola, Florida revival was initiated under the ministry of Steve Hill, an evangelist and church planter in Argentina for many years. He first heard of the revival at Holy Trinity Brompton, an Anglican congregation of London. Hill, traveled to London where he was prayed for. However, he says, he first received prayer while being a church planter in Argentina, by "15 or 20 people" prior to coming to Pensacola and London, including by Carlos Annacondia, an evangelist of the Argentine revival.⁶²

Instrumental in the impact of NACs in the United States has been Silvoso's ministry, Harvest Evangelism. Silvoso's ministry, considered as an "inter-denominational ministry," is fully committed to helping the churches in the fulfillment of the Great Commission. Silvoso first developed his city prayer evangelism strategy while in Argentina in the city of Resistencia, a project that took three years, and which culminated with

---

59. Ibid.
60. Comiskey, *Groups of 12*, 136.
61. Wagner, "Revival Power: God Has Set His People 'A-Praying,'" 9–12.
62. Ibid., Grady, "When God Interrupts Your Agenda," 26–30.

a 102 percent growth among the churches of the city. He later published his strategy in the book *That None Should Perish*.[63] Nevertheless, Silvoso's ministry goes beyond the publication of his book. He began making short mission trips to Argentina taking people from the United States to a hands-on training institute, so that people involved can come back to their local churches to implement what they have learned. His ministry expands now throughout the United States and "from Hong Kong to South America to the United Kingdom."[64]

Effects of Networking and Globalization on NACs

As previously stated (see Chapter 5), networking was born out of people's needs not being fulfilled by traditional institutions. In turn, people within the institutional system began to look for answers outside, and when found, they began to share this information with those in need.[65]

Characteristic of networks is the relational style of relationships. There is no hierarchical government in a network, but what matters is the sharing of information and resources that help each part involved in the network toward a common goal. This also implies that authority does not depend on status or position, but instead, on relationships. It is based on charisma. It is charisma in both senses of the word: that is, in the biblical sense, as based on the spiritual gifts bestowed upon the individual, and in the sense of personal ability.[66]

Because NACs in their beginnings were Independent Charismatic churches, coming out of denominational affiliations, many decided to stay independent. Others were born as independent churches as a reaction to hierarchical denominationalism. For both types, networking with other similar churches was the practical answer to the problem of feeling a sense of loneliness and isolation. There is also the baby boomer factor. Most NACs are attractive to the baby boomer generation, and networking is also an "appropriate sociology of church government for this generation."[67]

---

63. Silvoso, *Than None Should Perish*.
64. "About us," in *www.harvestevang.org*, n.d.
65. Naisbitt, *Megatrends*, 213–15.
66. Ibid., Pousson, *Spreading the Flame*, 62; Gibbs, *ChurchNext*, 84.
67. Pousson, *Spreading the Flame*, 63.

The Emergence of New Apostolic Churches 123

As a sociological answer to the problem of isolation, as well as an answer to the problem of identity, many NACs have opted to network with other churches. A "high-profile charismatic leader" whose ministry is considered to have apostolic dimensions usually leads these networks. In the case of the first century, many new churches were planted in pagan contexts, and led by relatively new converts who needed someone to guide him or her in the ministry. Apostles helped this kind of newly formed ministries by guiding people through oral teachings or letters with the "guarantee of authenticity." In today's NACs, although the first century scenario cannot be duplicated, there still are some ministers who "benefit from the leadership of biblically literate and spiritually mature pastors."[68] On the other hand, this brings many congregations under the leadership of one person. Not being able to assume leadership of such a geographically extended region, consequently leads to the formation of apostolic networks.[69]

An apostolic network is the gathering together of NACs (sometimes independent churches as well as denominational ones) and different ministries, "voluntary united in an organized structure" under the leadership or "covering" of an apostolic figure. Apostolic networks are different from denominations; because in a denomination there are policies and rules, there are legal and formal ties that bind churches and people together. In the case of a network what binds people are relationships. There are spiritual bonds, there is a common vision and goals, strategy and values, theological convictions, "and similar philosophies of ministry."[70]

Although many NACs network in a national scale involving sometimes thousands of churches, many others network in a global way. One example of this is the International Communion of Charismatic Churches, led by an international group of leaders from the United States, Brazil, Nigeria and the Caribbean. Most of the networks in the American Continent have connections overseas, reaching Africa as is the case of "the publications of Christian Growth Ministries" in South Africa, or the Vineyard movement cooperating in Johannesburg. However, in many

---

68. Gibbs, *ChurchNext*, 77.

69. Pousson, *Spreading the Flame*, 65, 70.

70. Cannistraci, *Apostles and the Emerging Apostolic Movement*, 190; see also Pousson, *Spreading the Flame*, 66; Gibbs, *ChurchNext*, 77.

cases churches that network together in other countries are the ones that seek connections with America.[71]

This kind of global networking is especially important with respect to the mission of the church. In the era of globalization, NACs also feel the effects of "missiological globalization." This is a very important development, because missiological globalization is the process that takes place when NACs network together to send missionaries to other countries. However, the idea of sending and receiving countries does not figure anymore, because "there is only a missionary network" that includes both, sending and receiving ends, sharing resources of any kind—spiritual, human, and economic, "to the most effective achievement of the mission of God."[72] Missionary networking is the result of unity among diversity. In a missionary network, churches bring their resources together toward a common goal, where a common understanding exists of one's own abilities as well as others' abilities where one lacks. Therefore, each member of the missionary network must understand that it is part of a team, where the joining together of all parts makes the network "with the whole being greater than the sum of the parts."[73-74]

Christians have always been characterized by taking the message of God traveling the world. In their traveling, they promote their "religious culture," people and objects of importance within the faith that can be considered as "contemporary manifestations of age-old proselytizing practices." This implies that globalization is nothing less than an amplification rather than a transformation "of human activity," when one compares the traditional pilgrimage many Christians have taken and are taking to religious sites, breaking any barriers and seeing no borders as

---

71. Poewe, "Introduction," 5–6.

72. Deiros, "From Renewal to Revival," 7.

73. Gibbs, *ChurchNext*, 89.

74. Edward Pousson gives some examples of how networking functions in the sending of missionaries. Pousson deals with the subject in two different chapters. One is dedicated to local congregations as missionary sending and the other one with new patterns of missionary agencies. In the latter, Pousson explains how charismatic churches join efforts to recruit, train, send, and supervise missionaries. Examples of these are the Gulf States Mission Agency and Living Water Teaching. Another type is the "extra-local mission structure," which, in light of the present study, is of great importance: the formation of "apostolic teams," to establish churches and leaders, as well as "to raise up, train and appoint" new leaders for the new church plant (Pousson, *Spreading the Flame*, 94–133).

obstacles in their journey. In today's globalized worldview, Christians have a wider "understanding of territory, society and cultural identity."[75]

The use of media in communicating the Gospel has had an effect in the global character of NACs. Along with networking, NACs have taken advantage of technological advances in furthering the faith, by using tools such as television, faxes, computers, and jet traveling. This is also seen in the impact of NACs as organizations, which in the era of globalization don't see borders in spreading the faith.[76] As Karla Poewe says, NACs "have become a global culture" because of their way of life which is spread through the use of "high-tech media; international conferences, fellowships, and prayer links; and mega-churches." In the case of mega-churches, these "function like international corporations" that export their faith through the print media, videos, or audiotapes to other network related congregations.[77]

---

75. Coleman, *The Globalization of Charismatic Christianity*, 4–5.
76. Ibid., 66.
77. Poewe, "Introduction," xi.

7

Conclusions

THE HISTORY OF THE church in mission is a very complicated and extensive subject, difficult to deal with in such a brief study. However, as the title of the book states, it is only a survey of the church's self-understanding of being the church and of mission, dealing briefly with the different epochs of the church in mission up to the last decade of the twentieth century leading to the emergence of New Apostolic Churches.

A surface level reading of church history will let us see how the church has changed throughout the centuries since her formation. However, as I have found out through this research, there are several factors that contributed to the paradigm shifts in the church's self-understanding of being the church and of mission. These factors are: Cultural, Christological, Pneumatological, Ecclesiological, Eschatological, and Missiological.

CULTURAL FACTORS THAT AFFECTED PARADIGM SHIFTS

The change process begins when basic assumptions, values, commitments, and allegiances are questioned. The big change in the church has always been that of changing her cultural perspective according to the present reality.

Paradigms begin to change at the deep level of culture, affecting the roots of culture, culminating with a paradigm shift—a totally new perspective of how reality is viewed or conceived. Changes in allegiance affect the change in worldview. This, for example, is the case of the church, changing her allegiance from Jesus Christ as resurrected savior to that of Jesus Christ within the empire, and back again to Jesus Christ resurrected.

The Christological Factor

The different concepts of Christ within Christianity are also factors that affected the church's self-understanding of being the church and of mission. As I found in the present research, in the beginning the church of the Apostolic Paradigm did not have problems in understanding the Christ of the crucifixion and the Christ of the resurrection.

Even though Docetism was confronted by the early apologists, Docetism has always been present, in some way, within the church. This is that when Christ is understood only as a person to be studied and defended, as the case of some apologists who live within the Christendom Paradigm, instead of a person with whom we can have a personal relationship, then the concept of the church as well as the concept of mission will be affected.

If Christ is not a real and always present person living among his people, then there is no reason for mission. If the concept of *Missio Dei* is to be practiced, then the concept of Christ must also be clarified. When the church considers Christ as a real and active person who dwells among his people, then the church meets to celebrate his resurrection, instead of only remembering his death.

As with the later developments of Christianity, the New Apostolic Paradigm has shown the concept of Christ as being restored to that of a living and always present divine person. When Christ is understood as a living person living among and indwelling his people, then the concept of the church will also be affected, because now the church understand herself as the body of Christ not a mystical one, but his living presence among the people.

The Pneumatological Factor

The concept of the Holy Spirit is also a determining factor in the different paradigms of Christianity. When the Holy Spirit was conceived of as a person who was called to help and be with the believer, the church prospered in fulfilling her mission.

During the Apostolic Paradigm, the Holy Spirit was considered as the *dunamis* of God, the ever-present power of God who enabled the believer to be effective in witnessing of the resurrected Christ. The Holy Spirit helped in accomplishing the mission because people would receive the Gospel, not because of the eloquence of the speakers, but because believers expected signs and wonders to follow the proclamation of the Gospel.

Sadly, controversies about the procession of the Holy Spirit diminished the divine person to a doctrine to be studied. During Christendom Paradigm, the Holy Spirit became a doctrine that needed to be defended. There is no problem with having a sound doctrine whatsoever, but it becomes a problem when believers begin to try to understand the Holy Spirit with their minds instead of considering him as a divine counselor always present.

During Christendom Paradigm, because the empire and the institutional church were seen as one and the same, the Holy Spirit was not the *dunamis* of God necessary to take the mission. The power during Christendom became the military power of the Empire. Gifts of the Spirit were confined to the clergy and became a matter of study.

Nevertheless, in these last decades of Christianity, the New Apostolic Paradigm, the church has seen an awakening of the Holy Spirit. The church does not only study about the Spiritual gifts, but also practices them. There has been an awakening in the spiritual gifts, a generalization of the Holy Spirit experience and emphasis on the manifestation of the power of God. There is a strong emphasis on a generalization of a Holy Spirit experience. That is, that every believer is encouraged and expected to have a Holy Spirit experience as well as to live under the anointing of the Holy Spirit for service and for effective witness. This Holy Spirit experience is not a once in a lifetime experience; they experience several fillings of the Spirit, which they call "the anointing." The anointing is not the same as the baptism with the Holy Spirit, as the Pentecostal tradition teaches, but it is an enabling of the believer by the Holy Spirit to accomplish God's mission through his or her life. Therefore, believers in NACs are also expected to ask for different kinds of anointing according to the need.

There is also an awakening of spiritual gifts. This does not mean that traditional or denominational churches do not believe in the gifts of the Spirit. If they do, they are to be studied and not actually practiced. Although some are Cessationists,[1] others do believe in the gifts of the Spirit as active and present. However, the major difference with NACs is that NACs encourage believers to find their spiritual gifts and develop

---

1. Cessationists are those believers who, according to their doctrine, believe the gifts of the Spirit ceased to exist or stopped after the original twelve apostles died.

them for the profit of the church. Spiritual gifts are not confined to the clergy or selected groups, but they are for all the people of God and are the means to effectively fulfill the mission of God.

The Ecclesiological Factor

Probably the most important factor is the ecclesiological one. It is out of the ecclesiology of the church that her mission will also be determined. During the first years of the church, it was mostly considered as a Jewish sect. With time, the church began to expand itself into the Gentile frontier.

The first generation of believers, as well as those who followed in the steps of the original apostles, did not have many problems in understanding their position and what they were supposed to do. Their worldview was set on the teachings of Christ and the apostles and prophets. In the early stages of Christianity, the church was a charismatic community. The church was a community where everybody had a God-given gift for the profit of the whole body. They lived in a hostile environment and understood that their primary mission was to be the hands, the eyes, the feet, and the heart of God in their community. They knew the instance they were out of the meeting place they stepped into the mission field.

However, when the church becomes an institution, everything changes. This is the case of the Christendom Paradigm. There is nothing wrong with being an institution, but the problem during Christendom is the fact that the church has come from being a living organism to an institutionalized organization.

In this face, the church builds herself from the inside, strengthening her foundations, and developing dogmas. The problem with this kind of ecclesiology is that the church enters the inward looking state, setting aside her mission to the world around. Life in the church is manifested by the developing of theology as opposed to the indwelling presence of Christ.

The New Apostolic Paradigm reflects a tendency towards a New Testament ecclesiology. This is an awakening of the need to resemble more and more the New Testament teachings of what the church is. This is, in fact, seen in the recent developments in the restoration of the government gifts of prophet and apostle, also in the similitude of the charismatic community of the Apostolic Paradigm.

Leadership roles are also affected by ecclesiology. The clergy and laity concepts are developments of the Christendom Paradigm, however, later developments show that these concepts, even though used within the New Apostolic Paradigm, only reflect a way of speaking about the salary-based ministry and the voluntary ministry. There is still a need to develop new terminology or to change our way of addressing the ministry.

Leaders are not the center of the church; they are the servants of all. A servanthood spirit is among the church. This brings about a change in the structure of the church, from being a hierarchical organization to a spiritual gift network. The people of God bring together their God-given gifts in order to effectively accomplish God's mission.

NACs think of every believer as a priest who intercedes for others before God, and before the people on behalf of God. Church pastors empower all believers to do the work of the ministry, which includes, among other things; visiting and praying for the sick, evangelizing the lost, calling last Sunday's guests, creating community, and acting upon one's spiritual gift to minister to others.

Another important finding with respect to ecclesiology is authority in NACs. Spiritual authority is achieved by spiritual parenthood expressed through mentoring relationships, rather than positional authority gained by one's job title. NACs develop mentoring relationships through small groups or cell groups. Many of them use small groups to create community and to minister to the saints. Nevertheless, the main emphasis of cell groups is for evangelism, ministry to people, and pastoral care. The idea behind cell groups is to be a large enough congregation to impact the city but small enough to care personally for everyone within the church.

Cell groups among NACs also show a restructuring of the church. The church does not rest upon one person or group of people (a board or committee), but on the many cell group leaders who care for all believers. In this way the ministry of the church is not centered on a superstar pastor or minister, but on all believers who also have access to God. The pastor's role then shifts to becoming the one who equips believers for ministry (Eph 4:11–12).

The Eschatological Factor

Eschatology has played an important role in the mission of the church, as well as how the church understands herself. Within the eschatological factors that affected the church are the resurrection of Christ and the coming of Christ.

When the church focuses on the resurrection of Christ, a sense of hope develops within the worshiping community. This is a hope for a new life, hope of the resurrection of all believers, because Christ is the first fruit. There is also the blessed assurance of Christ's return to reign among his people. This hope in the resurrection and the return of Christ also brings a spirit of celebration in the church. Each time the church gathers it is to celebrate the soon return of Christ.

Eschatology is also an important factor in the mission of the church, because it drives the church to fulfill the mission of God. When the church realizes the fact that Christ is coming back, the church finds a new zeal to reach the lost. This in turns helps in developing a new hermeneutics, as is the case with the New Apostolic Paradigm. This is a new way of interpreting the present considering the future presented by Scriptures, reading the signs of the times, and moving the church to a faster speed in accomplishing the mission.

The Missiological Factor

Twentieth-century developments have also change the concept of mission and missions. The developments of the *Missio Dei* and the *Missiones Ecclesiae* have also helped in understanding the concept of mission. A difference in what the purpose of the church is and how it must be accomplished is very important.

The greatest struggle of the church has always been that of balancing mission: that of building itself up and that of reaching the world without being of the world. Although there have been different changes in direction, power struggles, and difficult times of change and confusion, the focus has been the mission.

Missiology has been understood in different ways, and each one has accomplished the church specific purpose for a specific period of time. Mission during the Apostolic Paradigm was considered as the extension of Jesus' ministry. The church was to continue the redemptive work of Christ as its body on earth. However, during Christendom, missiology came to be understood in different ways, such as Christianization during the time of the crusades, colonization along with Christianization during the period of the Spanish and British empires, for example, and modernization during the era known as the "modern missions era."

However the concept of mission the church has in different epochs, the church has accomplish its mission. Nevertheless, we must ask ourselves if by Christianizing people we are fulfilling the Great Commission? Is colonization the right method of making disciples of every nation? Is bringing our modern culture, western culture to be more precise, the answer to the divine commandment?

ON THE EMERGENCE OF NACS

Renewal movements throughout the history of the church have helped the church maintain its vitality, and most of all, its vision and mission in focus. This has resulted in the emergence of cutting edge congregations, whose main focus is to carry the mission of God, and to live out as close as possible the New Testament pattern of being the church.

Nevertheless, this is not, and has not, been an easy task. Even from the beginning of the church, problems began to arise with respect to their mission. Jesus himself did not have as his mission the establishment of a new religion, to the point that he never left a credo, or a name for the movement. He came to establish the kingdom of God; but with time his followers grew in consciousness of what separated them from others, and the result was the church. What was supposed to be a movement became an institution. As Bosch points out, there are differences between a movement and an institution. A movement is progressive, while an institution is passive; a movement is aggressive and takes risks, while an institution longs for things; a movement crosses borders, an institution sees barriers. Nevertheless, the tendency to opt for an institution grew larger, to the point that there were two different types of ministry: the more sedentary one of the bishops and deacons, and the itinerant one of the apostles, prophets, and evangelists. The first one pulled the church toward institutionalization, while the other moved it in the dynamic of a movement.[2]

In the last two decades of the twentieth century, the church has experienced dramatic changes. In the trilogy, the word, the world, and the church, each one of them affects each other in some way. The word affects the church in her understanding and application of it; the church also

---

2. Bosch, *Misión en Transformación*, 73–74.

affects the world in fulfilling the mission of God; and the world affects both, the word and the church.

It is in the last part of the trilogy that renewal movements take place. The world affecting the church does not mean worldliness, but it has to do with how the church perceives the world in order to be relevant in doing her mission. In the last two decades of the twentieth century, the world has changed from modernity to postmodernity, and all of the effects of postmodernism have reached the church's ranks.

Postmodernity rejects the institutional, as well as the scientific reasoning, tending to be more experiential. Postmodern society is very pragmatic and individualistic, however, this does not mean isolation, but it values individual opinions. In relation to the church, postmodernism has its effects in the way worship is considered, seeking to provide a spiritual experience, rather than a rational one.

Globalization and networking are also developments of the 1980s and 1990s. Although they began in the 1970s, they found a more proliferated expression in the last two decades of the century. Along with this comes the post-institutional era, as a result of globalization and networking.

The secular events of the 1980s and 1990s affected the church, setting the stage for what happened in the religious arena. As the end of the millennium approached, a global revival began to take place. However, it is not a Christian global revival, but it has to do with a spiritual hunger in people, being met by different religious movements, the New Age movement being one result of postmodernity.

From the Christian perspective, the Holy Spirit revival of the early 1901 and 1906 saw its afterglow in the outpouring of the Spirit resulting in the Charismatic Movement of the 1960s. The 1980s saw another outpouring of the Spirit among traditional historic denominations, which, not wanting to be associated with the Pentecostal and the Charismatic movements, became known, as the Third Wave or Signs and Wonders movement. Churches experiencing opposition from their denominational peers, decided to become independent, birthing the Independent Charismatic Movement.

From the Third Wave and the Independent Charismatic movement, emerges the Neo-Charismatics. Not completely new, nevertheless, they understand that the Charismatic movement of the 1960s is over, and that God is working something new among the church. The combination of the last three movements gives birth to the postdenominational era, giving birth to the post-denominational church. However, the name became controversial, especially among traditional denominational leaders who reacted against it, until Wagner finally settled for the name New Apostolic Churches and called the movement New Apostolic Reformation.

Some important figures, who, through their research and writing helped in understanding the changes, are Lyle Schaller, Donald Miller, and C. Peter Wagner. The Spiritual Warfare movement and the cell group movement also play important roles in the emergence of NACs. Because of the emphasis on spiritual warfare and its role in evangelism in combination with cell groups, both for growth and pastoral care, many NACs have developed into mega-churches.

In this study I also found that NACs are not made in the USA. They are a Holy Spirit development throughout the world. Expressions of NACs are found in majority world countries: in South Africa, with the African-Initiated Churches, in China with the house church movement, and in Latin America with the grassroots churches.

The impact of such innovative congregations in the United States has been both positive and negative. The negative reaction considers that NACs are nothing other than a new global church, as the one depicted in the book of Revelation. On the other hand, the positive reaction comes from the fact that NACs have as their central focus the lost, the unchurched peoples, and with this in mind, NACs find new ways to reach them, locally and through foreign missions.

RECOMMENDATIONS

The church will always change. The reason for the always changing is that it is a living organism. However, we as believers play a very important role in the changing of the church because we are the church. When Christians change, the church also changes. It is with no doubt that changes are part of life, but the fear of change is what makes change so difficult. To be more precise, the fear of the unknown future is what makes the change more difficult.

The common phrase among believers is that we must go back to the Bible. This kind of statement has several implications. In order to be a Bible-based church, we must also be able to live according to the New Testament concept of the church and not what we think is the right concept. The New Testament church is one that sees herself as the extension of the ministry of Jesus Christ, his body on earth, his living presence to manifest his life, his power, and his love.

Based on the present study, I think that what we are seeing with the emergence of the New Apostolic Paradigm is the self-conscience of the church; that traditional views of the church as a body must be translated into a practical reality. The church has been endowed with the Holy Spirit to take advantage of the *dunamis* of God so we can be effective in a hostile and pagan world that doesn't ask anymore who is God, but how is he different from other gods?

Structural changes are in order too. This means that the church must change from a hierarchical structure to that of a body structure. In a hierarchy, leadership levels are from top to bottom, and authority is positional. If the church is going to be the body of Christ, the structure must be that of a body, every part must do its job for the well being of the whole body. Authority in this kind of structure is not positional, but relational. It is based on the relationship of every member with each other to accomplish a task.

In an organic view of the church, that of the body of Christ, every member is necessary, however not indispensable. Indispensable means that the body cannot function without a specific part. The indispensable part of the body of Christ must be its head. The head of the church must be Christ Jesus, who is also its foundation.

Unity is necessary to be the body of Christ. This means unity among diversity. Unity does not mean uniformity. In the unity of the body every member does its part by ministering according to the God-given gifts. The same thing applies to local congregations. Each congregation works along others in a town, city, or country to fulfill the mission of God for that specific place. Networking is the key factor in this kind of mission, and the expansion of the kingdom of God is the goal.

MINISTRY APPLICATION

As varied as the factors that produced the different paradigms of Christianity are, ministry applications are varied too. However, two are the most important ones that emerge from this study: the intra-denominational, and the global impact of the study.

Intra-Denominational Impact of the Study

Denominationalism is the result of Christendom. To be more exact, denominations are the fruit of dissension, the result from division of doctrine and practice. Even though churches come together under the same banner of doctrine and goals, there will always be a seed of dissension in them.

The problem with denominationalism is that instead of accomplishing the mission of God, denominations fulfill their own mission. The church exists with the purpose of bringing glory to God; however, the denominational game of power struggle does not glorify God, nor fulfill the mission.

On the Understanding of the Matter

If denominations are to be successful in the mission of God, denominations must be willing to change. Based on the present study, the future of denominations as we know them is very short. This does not mean that denominations will die or disappear, but denominationalism will. The church is moving beyond denominationalism, breaking the barriers of the denominational banner to raise the Christian banner.

Gifts of the Spirit must be present at all levels of leadership. The church must understand that change begins when as a body everyone does its part. Churches must unite to glorify God through mission. Denominational leaders should have an apostolic ministry; the name of the denomination must be secondary to the name of the Lord. Even though the future is unknown and the fear of an unknown future intimidates people, we must trust God and live according to the biblical mandate.

As was the case of the first century church, two different types of ministries developed, bishops and deacons pulling towards institutionalization and apostles, prophets and evangelists, pulling towards the dynamics of a movement. However, both types of ministries are necessary for the well being of the church.

The church as the body of Christ is made of many members, which are set in different positions in the body by the same Lord, and given the ability to work, by the same Spirit. Nevertheless, the important factor in the matter is how the church in the new millennium sees and understands the ministry gifts of Ephesians 4:11.

The church as an organism is always changing, but the change must always be towards the accomplishment of the mission of God. In order to accomplish the mission, the church must function with all of the ministry gifts in their right place, until we have grown to stature of the perfect man, Jesus Christ (Eph 4:13), who is the head of the church, and also the foundation on which it stands.

In the same way, I think that considering the period of time we are living in, Christian leaders have the responsibility to equip every member of the body in order to accomplish God's mission. Equipping the believer begins by accepting the role of an equipper. Every member must be taught to do the work of the ministry, in order to grow, not only spiritually, but also physically, which means to make disciples who reproduce into other disciples, making of every member a leader.

Global Impact of the Study

In a more global aspect, this study impacts the church by showing how we are living in Christendom, and how the church must move beyond Christendom in order to effectively accomplish her mission. As the study has shown, different factors affect the concept of the church and of mission.

Theological convictions of the church must change from being a matter of study to being a matter of practice. If the church believes in a resurrected Christ, then the church on a global level must witness the resurrection of Christ. Although Jesus' crucifixion is of importance without denial, his resurrection is of equal or greater importance. The church must celebrate the resurrected Christ, the soon coming Lord, and move beyond the remembering of the death and burial.

When the church gathers to celebrate Jesus' resurrection, then everything will change. There will be a sense of joy, a sense of hope, and a sense of life. By staying focused on Jesus' crucifixion, there is a feeling of sadness, despair, and death. The mission of the church is greatly affected by this kind of gathering of the worshipping community.

The church must see the New Apostolic Paradigm as a new stage in the life of the church in mission, and different to a new denomination. In the same way that we understand the Apostolic period or the Christendom period, we don't think of them as denominations, but as epochs in the life of the church. When we see the NAP as a new epoch in the life of the church in mission, then the paradigm shift will be smoother.

The NAP is also a new period in the life of the church, and if we, as the body of Christ, want to effectively accomplish the mission of God, must prepare ourselves to transition into this period, which is not of human conception, but as a result of the indwelling presence of the Spirit in the church. The better prepared we are, the sooner the transition will be. Whether we accept the change or not, the new paradigm is coming and soon the church will be embodied by it.

Nevertheless, the danger of enclosing the movement into traditional views still exists. Examples of this enclosing are: the Pentecostal, the Charismatic, or the Latter Rain Movements. The best way to prevent this is by understanding the NAP as an epoch in the life of the church; by a renewed understanding of the present reality of our mission frontier, our neighborhood; and by a restructuring of the church in order to be relevant to our present reality.

It is worth noting the fact that the New Apostolic Reformation is a very amorphous movement, not cohesive like the Pentecostal or the Charismatic Movements. Yet, another danger is the franchising of the movement. The emergence of several apostolic networks creates the danger of franchising, that is, of a multiplication of apostolic networks that will end up in denominations of the new paradigm, instead of multiplication of networks.

The New Apostolic Reformation is a reformation of structures, not the beginning of the birth of a new breed of several denominations. However, apostolic networks may fall into the temptation of becoming denominations when, or if, they begin to develop network affiliation policies and procedures, doctrinal statements, ordination requirements, and several other affiliation requirements similar to those of traditional denominationalism.

The New Apostolic Reformation is a restructuring of the church; it is an ecclesiological reformation. In the NAP people unite by a common vision; the main characteristic of the time is unity of vision, not uniformity.

On a More Personal Level

On a more personal level, I have seen the different changes that took place within the ranks of the church and how they affected the view of the church herself and of her mission in the world. I have seen how every epoch of Christianity has had its purpose in time. This means, that without doubt, the church fulfills her mission according the reality of the time the church lives in.

A very important aspect that I found is the vital role of every believer in fulfilling God's mission. Everybody has a very important part in the mission of God, and I think that the Reformation gave us in the present a very useful accomplishment, the ministry of all believers. It has taken some time for the church to put it into practice, however it is working.

As a pastor leading a congregation, I understand that my role is that of teaching the people of God to understand their mission in the world, and help them to find their place in the body according to the gift or gifts with which they have been endowed. This study has helped me in fine-tuning my ministry and my mission as a student of the missional church to better provide the people of God with the necessary tools to accomplish their mission in the world, by living as close as possible to the New Testament pattern of being the church.

Bibliography

Arthur, Chris. *The Globalization of Communications: Some Religious Implications*. Geneva: World Council of Churches, 1998.
Baker, Joel Arthur. *Future Edge Discovering the New Paradigms of Success*. New York: Morrow, 1992.
Barnhart, Robert K. "Paradigm." In *The Barnhart Dictionary of Etymology*. Edited by Robert K. Barnhart, H.W. Company, 1988.
Berg, Mike and Paul Pretiz. *The Gospel People of Latin America*. Monrovia, CA: MARC, World Vision International, 1992.
Bettenson, Henry, ed. *Documents of the Christian Church*. New York: Oxford University Press, 1967.
Blumhofer, Edith L. "Assemblies of God," In *Dictionary of Pentecostal and Charismatic Movements*, edited by Stanley M. Burgess, et al., 23-24. Grand Rapids: Zondervan, 1988.
Bosch, David J. *Transforming Mission: Paradigm Shifts in Theology of Mission* [Misión en Transformación: Cambios de Paradigma en la Teología de la Misión]. Maryknoll, NY: Orbis, 1991.
―――. *Misión en Transformación: Cambios de Paradigma en la Teología de la Misión* [Transforming Mission: Paradigm Shift in Theology of Mission]. Maryknoll, NY: Libros Desafío, 2000.
Bottari, Pablo. "Dealing With Demons in Revival Evangelism." In *The Rising Revival: Firsthand Accounts of the Incredible Argentine Revival—And How it can Spread Throughout the World*, edited by C. Peter Wagner and Pablo A. Deiros, 75-90. Ventura, CA: Renew, 1998.
Boyd, Gregory A. *God at War: The Bible and Spiritual Conflict*. Downers Grove, IL: InterVarsity, 1997.
Bromiley, Geoffrey W. *Historical Theology: An Introduction*. Grand Rapids: Eerdmans, 1978.
Bruner, Frederick Dale. *A Theology of the Holy Spirit: The Pentecostal Experience and the New Testament Witness*. Grand Rapids: Eerdmans, 1970.
Burgess, Stanley M., et al, eds. "The Pentecostal and Charismatic Movements." In *Dictionary of Pentecostal and Charismatic Movements*. Grand Rapids: Zondervan, 1988.
Cairnes, Earle E. *Christianity Through the Centuries*. 2nd rev. ed. Grand Rapids: Zondervan, 1981.

Castellanos, Cesar. *Sueña y Ganarás al Mundo* [Dream and You Will Win the World]. Bogotá, Colombia: Vilit, 1998.

Castro, Emilio. *Sent Free: Mission and Unity in the Perspective of the Kingdom.* Geneva: World Council of Churches, 1985.

Campolo, Tony. *Can Mainline Denominations Make a Comeback?* Valley Forge, PA: Judson, 1995.

Cannistraci, David. *Apostles and the Emerging Apostolic Movement.* Ventura, CA: Renew, 1996.

Coleman, Simon. *The Globalization of Charismatic Christianity.* Cambridge: Cambridge University Press, 2000.

Comiskey, Joel. *Home Cell Group Explosion: How Your Small Group Can Grow And Multiply.* Houston, TX: TOUCH, 1998.

———. *Groups of 12: A New Way to Mobilize Leaders and Multiply Groups in Your Church.* Houston, TX: TOUCH, 1999.

Cho, Paul Yonggi. *Los Grupos Familiares y el Crecimiento de la Iglesia* [Successful Home Cell Groups]. Deerfield, FL: Vida, 1982.

Damazio, Frank. *Seasons of Revival: Understanding the Appointed Times of Spiritual Refreshing.* Portland, OR: BT Pub, 1996.

De Carvalho, Levi T. "The Shaman and the Missionary: Worldview Construction among the Terena." PhD diss., Fuller Theological Seminary, 1999.

Deiros, Pablo A. and Carlos Mraida. *Latinoamérica en Llamas* [Latin America in Flames]. Miami, FL: Caribe, 1994.

Deiros, Pablo A. *Protestantismo en América Latina: Ayer, Hoy y Mañana* [Protestantism in Latin America: Yesterday, Today and Tomorrow]. Nashville, TN: Caribe, 1997.

———. "The Roots and Fruits of the Argentine Revival." In *The Rising Revival: Firsthand Accounts of the Incredible Argentine Revival—And How it can Spread Throughout the World,* edited by C. Peter Wagner and Pablo A. Deiros, 29–57. Ventura, CA: Renew, 1998.

———. "From Renewal to Revival." Class syllabus for MC558. Pasadena, CA: Fuller Theological Seminary, 2001.

Delph, Ed. "Unleashing God's Power in Your City." *Ministries Today,* Jan–Feb, 1996. 27–31.

Dunn, James D. G. "Models of Christian Community in the New Testament." In *Strange Gifts?: A Guide to Charismatic Renewal,* edited by David Martin and Peter Mullen, 1–18. New York: Blackwell, 1984.

Dussel, Enrique. *History and the Theology of Liberation.* Translated by John Drury. Maryknoll, NY: Orbis, 1976.

———. *Historia General de la Iglesia en América Latina,* Tomo 1 [General History of the Church in Latin America, Vol. 1]. Salamanca: Sígueme, 1983.

Easum, William. *Dancing with Dinosaurs: Ministry in a Hostile and Hurting World.* Nashville, TN: Abigndon, 1993.

Encarta Encyclopedia. "Change, Christendom, Catalyst, Post." CD-ROM, 1999.

Finnell, David. *Life in His Body: A Simple Guide to Active Cell Life.* Houston, TX: TOUCH, 1995.

Grady, J. Lee. "When God Interrupts Your Agenda: An Interview with the Leaders of Brownsville Assembly of God." *Ministries Today,* Nov–Dec, 1996. 26–30.

Grassie, William. "Postmodernism: What One Needs to Know." *Zygon* 32:1 (1997) 83–94.

Gibbs, Eddie. *ChurchNext: Quantum Change in How We Do Ministry.* Downers Grove, IL: InterVarsity, 2000.

González, Justo L. *Historia del Cristianismo, Vol. 1* [History of Christianity, Vol. 1]. Miami, FL: Unilit, 1994.
Grenz, Stanley. *Theology for the Community of God*. Nashville, TN: Broadman and Holman, 1994.
Guthrie, Donald. *New Testament Introduction*. Downers Grove, IL: InterVarsity, 1990.
Hägglund, Bengt. *History of Theology*. Tranlated by Gene J. Lund. Saint Louis, MO: Concordia, 1968.
Harrison, Everett. *Introducción al Nuevo Testamento* [New Testament Introduction]. Translated by Norberto Wolf. Grand Rapids: Subcomisión de Literatura Cristiana de la Iglesia Cristiana Reformada, 1980.
Hexham, Irving and Karla Powe. "Charismatic Churches in South Africa: A Critique of Criticisms and Problems of Bias." In *Charismatic Christianity as Global Culture*. Edited by Karla Powe, 50–69. Columbia, SC: University of South Carolina Press, 1994.
Hiebert, Paul E. *Anthropological Reflections on Missiological Issues*. Grand Rapids: Baker, 1994.
Hinn, Benny. *Good Morning, Holy Spirit*. Nashville, TN: Thomas Nelson, 1990.
———. *The Anointing*. Nashville, TN: Thomas Nelson, 1990.
Hocken, Peter D. "Charismatic Movement." In *Dictionary of Pentecostal and Charismatic Movements*. Edited by Stanley M. Burgess et al., 130–60. Grand Rapids: Zondervan, 1988.
Hong, In Sik. *Una Iglesia Posmoderna? : En Busca de Un Modelo de Iglesia y Misión en la Era Posmoderna* [A Postmodern Church?: In Search of a Model of Church and Mission in the Postmodern Era]. Colección FTL, no. 9. Buenos Aires: Kairós, 2001.
Hurd, R. Wesley. "Postmodernism." McKenzie Study Center. http://mckenziestudycenter.org/2001/02/postmodernism/
Horton, Stanely M. *El Espíritu Santo Revelado en la Biblia* [The Holy Spirit Revealed in the Bible]. Miami, FL: Vida, 1980.
How Paradigm Shift. www.tapestry.org/paradigmshift/html (Accessed 2/9/2001).
Ignatius, *Epistle to the Ephesians*. In *Documents of the Christian Church*. Edited by Henry Bettenson. New York: Oxford University Press, 1967.
Kittel, Gerhard and Gerhard Friedrich, eds. "Dunamai, Dunamij." In *Theological Dictionary of the New Testament. Abridge in One volume*, translated by Geoffrey W. Bromiley. Grand Rapids: Eerdmans, 1985.
Kraft, Charles H. *Christianity in Culture: A Study in Dynamic Biblical Christianity in Cross-cultural Perspective*. Maryknoll, NY: Orbis, 1979.
———. *Christianity with Power: Your Worldview and Your Experience of the Supernatural*. Ann Arbor, MI: Servant, 1989.
———. *Anthropology for Christian Witness*. Maryknoll, NY: Orbis, 1996.
Küng, Hans. "What Does a Change of Paradigm Mean?" In *Paradigm Change in Theology*. Edited by Hans Küng and David Tracy, translated by Margaret Kohl, 212–19. New York: Crossroad, 1991.
Kuhn, Thomas S. *The Structure of Scientific Revolutions*. 2nd. ed. Chicago: University of Chicago Press, 1970.
Latourette, Kenneth Scott. *Historia del Cristianiasmo, Vol. 1* [History of Christianity, Vol. 1]. Translated by Jaime C. Quareles and Lemuel C. Quarles. 10th. Ed. El Paso, TX: Casa Bautista, 1997.

———. *Historia del Cristianismo*, Vol. 2 [History of Christianity, Vol. 2]. Translated by Jaime C. Quareles and Lemuel C. Quarles. 7th. ed. El Paso, TX: Casa Bautista, 1992.

Logan, Bob. *Beyond Church Growth*. Grand Rapids: Revell, 1989.

Martin, Ralph P. *The Four Gospels*, vol. 1, *New Testament Foundations: A Guide for Christian Students*. Grand Rapids: Eerdmans, 1975.

Mays, Patrick. "After Christendom, What?: Renewal and Discovery of Church and Mission in the West. *Missiology*. 27:2 (April 1999): 245–55.

Maxwell, John. *Desarrolle el Líder que Está en Usted* [Developing the Leader Within You]. Translated by Guillermo Vásquez. Nashville, TN: Caribe, 1996.

Mead, Loren B. *The Once and Future Church: Reinventing the Congregation for a New Mission Frontier*. New York: Alban Institute, 1991.

Miller, Donald E. *Reinventing American Protestantism: Christianity in the New Millennium*. Los Angeles: University of California Press, 1997.

Moriarty, Michael G. *The New Charismatics: A Concerned Voice Responds to Dangerous Trends*. Grand Rapids: Zondervan, 1992.

Mraida, Carlos. "Unity as a Sign of Revival." In *The Rising Revival: Firsthand Accounts of the Incredible Argentine Revival—And How it can Spread Throughout the World*. Edited by C. Peter Wagner and Pablo A. Deiros, 185–98. Ventura, CA: Renew, 1998.

Naisbitt, John. *Megatrends*. New York: Warner, 1984.

Naisbitt, John, and Patricia Aburdene, eds. *Megatrends 2000*. New York: Morrow, 1990.

Nissen, Johannes. "Paradigms of Mission in the Four Gospels." The University of Copenhagen Guest Lecture, Sept. 9. In Charles E. Van Engen "Biblical Foundations of Missions," Class Syllabus for MT520, 395–403. Pasadena, CA: Fuller Theological Seminary, 1996.

Oakley, Ed, and Doug Kroug. *Enlightened Leadership: Getting to the Heart of Change*. New York: Simon and Schuster, 1991.

O'Brien, Peter T. "Church." In *Dictionary of Paul and His Letters*. Edited by Gerald F. Hawthorne et al., 123–31. Downers Grove, IL: InterVarsity, 1993.

O'Conner, Edward D. *The Pentecostal Movement in the Catholic Church*. Notre Dame, IN: Ave Maria, 1971.

Ogden, Greg. *The New Reformation: Returning the Ministry to the People of God*. Grand Rapids: Zondervan, 1990.

"Our Calling." http://www.harvestevan.org/our-calling.html.

Padilla, C. René. *Mission between the Times*. Grand Rapids, MI: William B. Eerdmans, 1985.

Poewe, Karla. "Introduction: The Nature, Globality, and History of Charismatic Christianity." In *Charismatic Christianity as a Global Culture*. Edited by Karla Poewe, 1–29. Columbia, SC: University of South Carolina Press, 1994.

Pousson, Edward K. *Spreading the Flame: Charismatic Churches and Mission Today*. Grand Rapids: Zondervan, 1992.

Present Futures of the Church. www.ntcumc.org/ArcMyC/MyC9805.html. Edited by Robert L. Robertson, May–June.

Paige, Terrence. "Holy Spirit." In *Dictionary of Paul and His Letters*. Edited by Gerald F. Hawthorne et al., 404–13. Downers Grove, IL: InterVarsity, 1993.

Paradowski, Robert. "Paradigm and Theories." In *Survey of Social Science, Vol. 3*. Edited by Franklin N. Magill, 1328–35. Englewood Cliffs, NJ: Salem, 1994.

Pearlman, Myer. *A Través de la Biblia* [Through the Bible]. Miami, FL: Vida, 1952.

Perschbacher, Wesley J. ed. *The New Analytical Greek Lexicon*. Peabody, MA: Hendrickson, 1994.
Petersen, Jim. *Church Without Walls: Moving Beyond Traditional Boundaries*. Colorado Springs: Navepress, 1992.
Placher, Paul E. *A History of Christian Theology*. Philadelphia, PA: Westminster, 1983.
Quebedeaux, Richard. *The New Charismatics II*. San Francisco: Harper and Row, 1983.
Rainer, Thom S. *Giant Awakenings: Making the Most of 9 Surprising Trends That Can Benefit Your Church*. Nashville, TN: Broadman and Holman, 1995.
Regele, Mike and Mark Schulz. *Death of the Church*. Grand Rapids: Zondervan, 1996.
Robertson, Roland. "Globalization and the Future of Traditional Religion." In *Religion and the Powers of the Common Life*. Vol 1, *God and Globalization*. Edited by Max L. Stackhouse et al., 53–69. Harrisburg, PA: Trinity, 2000.
Roxburgh, Alan J. *The Missionary Congregation, Leadership and Liminality*. Harrisburg, PA: Trinity, 1997.
Silvoso, Ed. *That None Should Perish: How to Reach Cities for Christ through Prayer Evangelism*. Ventura, CA: Regal, 1994.
Schaller, Lyle, E. *The New Reformation: Tomorrow Arrived Yesterday*. Nashville, TN: Abigndon, 1995.
———. *The Seven-Day-A-Week Church*. Nashville, TN: Abingdon, 1997.
Shaw, R. Dan. "Introduction to Research Design." Class Syllabus for MB561. Pasadena, CA: Fuller Theological Seminary, 2000.
Sloyan, Gerard S. *The Jesus Tradition: Images of Jesus in the West*. Mystic, CT: Twenty Third, 1986.
Smart, Barry. "Modernity, Postmodernity and the Present." In *Theories of Modernity and Postmodernity*. Edited by Bryan S. Turner, 14–29. Thousand Oaks, CA: SAGE, 1990.
Smith, Ebbie. *The New Apostolic Church: Fad, Impractical, or Imperative?* www.swbts.edu/si/articles/apostolichrch.htm.
Snyder, Howard A. *Radical Renewal: The Problem of the Wineskins Today*. Houston, TX: TOUCH, 1996.
Stackhouse, Max L. "General Introduction." In *God and Globalization Vol. 1*. Edited by Max L. Stackhouse and Peter J. Paris, 1–52. Harrisburg, PA: Trinity, 2000.
Tenney, Merrill C. *Nuestro Nuevo Testamento: Estudio Panorámico del Nuevo Testamento* [Our New Testament: New Testament Survey]. Rev. ed. Grand Rapids: Portavoz, 1989.
The Third Reformed Church–Holland. "The Post-modern Culture." In *Adult Sunday School Class Syllabus*, 1990.
Tillin, Tricia, and Orrel Steinkamp. "The Second Pentecost Leads to the World Church." In *The Plumbline*. www.members.ozemal.com.au/~rseaborn/apostles.html.
Towns, Elmer. *Is the Day of the Denomination Dead?* Nashville, TN: Nelson, 1973.
———. "Foreword." In *The New Apostolic Churches*. Edited by C. Peter Wagner, 7–9. Ventura, CA: Regal, 1998.
Turner, Bryan S. "Periodization and Politics in the Postmodern." In *Theories of Modernity and Postmodernity*. Edited by Bryan S. Turner, 1–13. Thousand Oaks, CA: SAGE, 1990.
Trueblood, Elton. *La Iglesia: Un Compañerismo Incendiario* [The Incendiary Fellowship]. El Paso, TX: Casa Bautista, 1981.
Vallet, Ronald E., and Charles E. Zech. *The Mainline Church's Funding Crisis: Issues and Possibilities*. Grand Rapids: Eerdmans, 1995.

Van Engen, Charles E. *God's Missionary People: Rethinking the Purpose of the Local Church.* Grand Rapids, MI: Baker, 1991.

———. "Biblical Foundations of Mission." Class Syllabus for MT520. Pasadena, CA: Fuller Theological Seminary, 1998.

———. "Theologizing in Mission." Class Syllabus for MT837. Pasadena, CA: Fuller Theological Seminary, 2002.

Vos, Howard G. *Breve Historia de la Iglesia* [Brief History of the Church]. Grand Rapids: Kregel, 1988.

Wagner, C. Peter. "The Third Wave." In *Dictionary of Pentecostal and Charismatic Movements*, edited by Stanley M. Burgess et al., 844–45. Grand Rapids: Zondervan, 1988.

———. *The Third Wave of the Holy Spirit: Encountering the Power of Signs and Wonders Today.* Ann Arbor, MI: Servant, 1988.

———. *Strategies for Church Growth.* Ventura, CA: Regal, 1989.

———. "Those Amazing Postdenominational Churches." *Ministries Today*, Juy–Aug, 1994. 1–3.

———. "The New Paradigms of Today's Emerging Churches." *Ministries Today*, Mar–Apr, 1996. 51–55.

———. "Contemporary Dynamics of the Holy Spirit in Missions: A Personal Pilgrimage." Paper presented at the Triennial Meeting of IFMA/EFMA/EMS. Orlando, FL, September 20–23, 1996.

———. "The New Apostolic Reformation." In *The New Apostolic Churches*. Edited by C. Peter Wagner. 13–25. Ventura, CA: Regal, 1998.

———. "Revival Power: God Has Set His People 'A-Praying.'" In *The Rising Revival: Firsthand Accounts of the Incredible Argentine Revival—And How it can Spread Throughout the World.* Edited by C. Peter Wagner and Pablo A. Deiros, 7–27. Ventura, CA: Renew, 1998.

———. *Churchquake: How the New Apostolic Reformation is Shaking up the Church as we Know it.* Ventura, CA: Regal, 1999.

W.E. Vine, *Diccionario Expositivo de Palabras del Nuevo Testamento, Vol. M–S* [Expositive Dictionary of New Testament Words, Vol. M–S]. (Barcelona, España: CLIE, 1984), 106–7.

Williams, J. Roadman. "Baptism in the Holy Spirit." In *Dictionary of Pentecostal and Charismatic Movements*, edited by Stanley M. Burgesset al., 40–48. Grand Rapids: Zondervan, 1988.

Witerington, Ben III. "Christology." In *Dictionary of Paul and His Letters*. Edited by Gerald F. Hawthorne, Ralph P. Martin, and Daniel Reid, 100–115. Downers Grove, IL: InterVarsity, 1993.

Wuthnow, Robert. *Christianity in the Twenty-First Century: Reflections on the Challenges Ahead.* New York: Oxford University Press, 1993.

www.ingramcontent.com/pod-product-compliance
Lightning Source LLC
Chambersburg PA
CBHW060915190426
43197CB00012BA/2510